DATE			
MAR 27 80			

The Language of the Railroader

THE LANGUAGE OF THE RAILROADER

by
Ramon F. Adams, 1889-1976.

University of Oklahoma Press : Norman

Books by Ramon F. Adams

Cowboy Lingo (Boston, 1936)
Western Words: A Dictionary of the Range, Cow Camp, and Trail (Norman, 1944)
Charles M. Russell, the Cowboy Artist (with Homer E. Britzman) (Pasadena, 1948)
Come an' Get It: The Story of the Old Cowboy Cook (Norman, 1952)
The Best of the American Cowboy (compiler and editor) (Norman, 1957)
The Rampaging Herd: A Bibliography of Books and Pamphlets on Men and Events in the Cattle Industry (Norman, 1959)
A Fitting Death for Billy the Kid (Norman, 1960)
The Old-Time Cowhand (New York, 1961)
Burs Under the Saddle: A Second Look at Books and Histories of the West (Norman, 1964)
From the Pecos to the Powder: A Cowboy's Autobiography (with Bob Kennon) (Norman, 1965)
The Legendary West (Dallas, 1965)
The Cowman and His Philosophy (Austin, 1967)
The Cowboy and His Humor (Austin, 1968)
Western Words: A Dictionary of the American West (Norman, 1968)
The Cowman and His Code of Ethics (Austin, 1969)
Six-Guns and Saddle Leather: A Bibliography of Books and Pamphlets on Western Outlaws and Gunmen (Norman, 1954; revised and enlarged edition, 1969)
The Language of the Railroader (Norman, 1977)

Library of Congress Cataloging in Publication Data

Adams, Ramon Frederick, 1889–1976.
  The language of the railroader.

  Includes bibliographical references.
  1. Railroads—Dictionaries. I. Title.
TF9.A32   625.1'003   77–22346

Dedicated to
Fred and Marguarite Grillo
with fond
good wishes

 # PREFACE

Practically every vocation in America has its own colorful language, and railroading is no exception. Like the language of the cowboy and of the logger, the railroader's jargon has greatly enriched our language. Much of it has been accepted by lexicographers and dictionary makers.

What older adult is there, remembering the trains of the days of steam, who does not have nostalgic memories of the huge, throbbing engines, the shining passenger cars, the uniformed trainmen, and the fascinating sounds of steam, bell, and whistle? After school small-town children rushed down the track to the station to see the train pull in. Boys longed for the day when they would grow up to become engineers. To them the driver of this monster was a sort of deity. The social center of the small town was the depot, where the natives could see people from the "outside" and the fascinating varnished passenger cars. Back in those days, when there were no radios or television for entertainment, a favorite pastime was gathering to see the trains, especially on Sundays.

Those of us who traveled the steam trains can remember the brakeman's announcements of the next stations as he came through the cars, waking the sleepers with his deep, clear voice; or the ringing of the dinner chimes with their melodious tones as the announcer walked up the aisle calling, "Dinner is now being served in the dining car at the rear"; or, after a stop at a station for passengers and the exchange of mail and express, the sight of the white-coated Pullman porter standing by his boxlike stool at the car steps smiling his welcome to passengers; or the engineer dressed in overalls and long-billed cap, descending from his cab at the station to oil the works of the engine with his long-spouted oil can.

There are also the memories of the dining-car chef leaning from his kitchen door in his tall hat and his white apron and jacket and, at night, the glistening lights as the train passed through small towns without stopping and the darkness of the country except for occasional dim, distant lights from the windows of farmhouses along the way. When the train stopped at a larger town, one heard the car inspectors ("car knockers") at their noisy work and saw the lanterns bobbing in and out between the cars as the trainmen examined the air and steam lines and the couplings.

There was something fascinating about trains even before the improvements of vestibules and screened windows, when it was dangerous to go from car to car. In the summer, before air conditioning, with raised windows it was unusual not to get cinders in one's eyes. After air conditioning arrived, there was the bumping and thumping of blocks of ice being placed in the cooling units at some division point. By that time, too, there were double-glassed windows and the vestibules with their Ajax diaphragms. In spite of the beauty of the all-steel diesel trains, there had been a greater fascination with the colossal steam engines with their huge drivers and clouds of black smoke trailing behind and their musical whistles as they blew for crossings or the approach to a station. Another fascinating sight was the fast through freight as it thundered through a small town, kicking up dust as it roared by, each car swaying in its own way. If the weather was good, one would likely see a brakeman sitting on a brake wheel, his hair flying in the breeze as he enjoyed the cooling wind. At night one could see faint objects down the track in the illumination of the headlight or the glow in the sky as the fireman opened his boiler door to feed in more coal. Often the engineer went through such towns late at night without a whistle to avoid waking the station agent or the citizens, for which consideration all were grateful. The unavoidable noise of the wheels on rails became more and more faint until the green lights on the rear of the caboose faded in the distance.

The railroader's colorful lingo was also fascinating to an outsider, though he might fail to comprehend its meaning. He might overhear two railroaders talking. One of them might say: "The crumb boss was flippin' his tissues on the angel's seat in the monkey house, the ash cat was usin' the blister end of his idiot stick to feed the hog black diamonds so the hogger would have fog enough to bat the stack off her after the rear shack took his brownie can and went back far enough with his bird cage to spike a torch while the head shack was coolin' a hot jewel up near the pig."

To an outsider this talk would be just so much foreign language, but to the railroader it meant that the conductor was reading his train orders while sitting in the cupola of the caboose; the fireman was shoveling coal to feed the engine fuel so that the engineer would have enough steam to make speed after the rear brakeman had taken his signal box with his lantern to throw a torch into a tie at the rear of the train; and the head brakeman was doctoring a hot box up near the engine.

As another example, a railroader might say: "On the northbound the brainless wonder juggled the circle from the lightning slinger, and the boss didn't know he was to put in the hole at Block's Siding. When the pig mauler saw the southbound right on him as they rounded a curve, he knew they were going to have a cornfield meet. He pulled the calf's tail once and yelled to his clinker boy to jump, and they both joined the birds. Soon after that the gandy dancers were building a shoofly around that pileup." A railroad man would know that a conductor missed a train-order hoop held by the telegraph operator and thus missed the order from the dispatcher to pull into Block's Siding. Then, when he saw a southbound train upon him as they rounded a curve, he realized that they were going to have a wreck and pulled the whistle cord, yelling to his fireman to jump. They both proceeded to do so, and shortly afterward the wrecking crew was building a temporary track around the wreck.

A stranger in a restaurant patronized by railroad men would be astounded by the language they gave the beanery queen, and more so by the orders she relayed to the cook. Eggs straight up were "with headlights." If they were to be fried over, the order was, "Blanket the headlights." Scrambled eggs were "wreck on the main line." A steak well done was a "hotbox asmokin'." All food was ordered by some railroad expression.

Now that there are no longer steam engines but diesels pulling freight trains a mile long and very few passenger trains, some of this picturesque language is being lost. Because of this I have prepared the following collection in an attempt to preserve it for posterity.

RAMON F. ADAMS

Dallas, Texas

The Language of the Railroader

accommodation train: Usually a *mixed train (q.v.)* running a short route for the convenience of its customers.

adhesion: The grip of the wheels on the rails, depending largely on the weight of the car or engine above them.

adverse: An uphill railroad grade.

advertised: Announced; referring to a time table, as "time as per *advertised* schedule."

age: Seniority; the length of an employee's service with the company.

air: Short for *air brake (q.v.)*.

air artist: A locomotive engineer skilled in the use of the *air brake (q.v.)*.

air brake: Any brake operated by air pressure, but usually restricted to a system of continuous brakes operated by compressed air, as distinguished from a vacuum brake; a brake operated by a piston driven by compressed air.

air-brake instruction car: A car, usually one converted from a passenger car, in which is mounted all of the apparatus necessary to illustrate and explain the construction and operation of all parts of the air brake. It is used to instruct railway employees, and the car is stationed at different places for short periods. Regular classes are held, with lectures by an expert.

air-brake tests: A code issued by a committee on air-brake tests, originated in 1895 to test the *triple valve (q.v.)*.

air car: A freight car equipped with air brakes.

air flue: A vertical shaft in a refrigerator car through which cold air passes to the refrigerator.

air gauge: A gauge to register the pressure of air in the reservoir, brake pipe, or brake cylinders, similar to an ordinary steam-pressure gauge. The gauge is made either with a single pointer or with two pointers to indicate on one dial both the reservoir pressure and the brake-pipe pressure. The latter gauge is called a *duplex gauge.*

air giver: A brakeman.

air inlet: An opening for the admission of air to an air compressor or a refrigerator car. It includes both the air strainer and the *air pipe (q.v.).*

air jammer: A worker who connects the air hoses on freight cars and the air signals and air hoses on passenger trains. In making up a train, though the cars are automatically coupled on contact, no freight cars are equipped with automatic couplings for steam hoses to carry air for brakes, steam heating, and signal equipment, and some passenger cars are not so equipped. The air jammer makes these connections. Also called *air jumper.*

air jumper: See *air jammer.*

air monkey: An air-brake repairman.

air pipe: A brake pipe; also called *train pipe.*

air pump and motor: A machine for compressing air, mounted beneath the floor of a car, composed of air cylinders whose pistons are gear-driven by a motor.

air-pump cylinder: A hollow, cast-iron cylinder with a piston that compresses the air required to operate the brakes. The pistons are joined by connecting rods to a crankshaft geared to a small motor.

air-pump cylinder head: The cover for the lower end of the air cylinder of a motor-driven air pump for air brakes.

air space: The insulating space between the linings of a refrigerator car. It is often called *dead-air space* to distinguish it from the ventilating passages, since the air is confined and not being constantly changed.

air valve: A small outlet valve that passes air but not water at the ends of storage heaters to allow the air to escape when steam or hot water is turned on.

ajax diaphragm: The cotton-fabric diaphragm for vestibules, composed of sections riveted at the joints and bound with leather at the corners. It is made in two styles, single for Pullman and double for Gould vestibules.

alcove faucet: A faucet in a passenger-car water alcove connected to a water cooler to supply drinking water.

alcove lamp: A lamp placed in the recess in the side of a passenger car. It was often called *panel lamp,* because it was usually covered with a panel.

Allegheny-type engine: A 2-6-6-6 locomotive introduced by the Chesapeake and Ohio Railroad in 1941.

alley: A clear track in a switching yard.

alleyway: A corridor. The narrow passage at the side of staterooms and compartments in sleeping and parlor cars.

alligator jaw: A connection on an interlocking switch.

all up: The expression of a train crew that has completed its work before quitting time.

amber signal: A light used at night (the same as a 45-degree position of the arm on a semaphore) signifying that the following block can be occupied.

ambulance: A caboose.

American-type engine: A 4-4-0 locomotive that first appeared in the 1830's.

anchor: A caboose.

anchor her: To set the brakes. To set hand brakes on a standing car.

anchor: A hand brake.

angel's seat: The cupola of a caboose.

angle cock: A cock placed in the brake pipe under each end of the car just in front of the hose connection. It is closed at the rear end of the last car to keep the air from escaping but must be open on all the other cars.

animal car: A caboose.

Annie Oakley: A railroad pass.

anvil: The interior piece of iron directly over the fulminating powder to ensure ignition for signals.

ape wagon: A caboose.

APPLY THE BRAKES
> *See* anchor, anchor her, big hole, clean the clock, club 'em down, give her the air, give her the one, give her the works, goose, horse her over, plug the engine, pull the air, pull the white cord, put it in the big hole, shoot the works, slug, squirrel a car, tie 'em down, tie the train down, wing her, wipe the chock, wipe the gauge.

apron: A flat metal platform between the locomotive and the tender.

armored brake hose: A brake hose covered with a heavy protective woven fabric.

arms horse car: A car especially designed for the transportation of valuable horses, fitted with removable partitions for stalls.

Armstrong: A locomotive that is not equipped with a stoker. Old-style equipment operated with muscles, such as the early turntable and hand brake.

articulated locomotive: A locomotive with two driving-wheel assemblies, each powered by a set of cylinders.

artist: A workman expert at his job; usually prefixed by *air*, *brake*, *speed*, and so on. Also, an incompetent worker, as *bailing-wire artist (q.v.)*.

asbestos: The trainman's word for coal that is hard to burn.

ash cat: A locomotive fireman.

ash eater: A fireman.

ash pit: A pit at a division point into which the ashes from the engines are dumped.

ash-pit engineer: Any workman (usually the fireman) who services engines, especially at division points and terminals.

at blowoff: Complete, ready; said of a safety valve that is ready to blow off steam when the boiler is at full pressure.

Atlantic-type locomotive: A 4-4-2 locomotive introduced in the 1880's.

atmospheric brake: The first brake operated by compressed air, invented by George Westinghouse in 1868; the predecessor of the *automatic air brake (q.v.)*.

atmospheric engine: An early low-pressure engine developed by Thomas Newcomen.

automatic air brake: A brake applied automatically, invented by George Westinghouse in 1871, the successor to the *atmospheric brake (q.v.)*.

auxiliary reservoir: A cylinder-shaped reservoir that holds the compressed air supplied by the main reservoir.

auxiliary tank: See *auxiliary reservoir*.

axle offset: A ridge formed by reducing the diameter of that part of an axle upon which a wheel turns, thus keeping the wheel from moving inward on the axle.

baby lifter: A passenger-train brakeman.

back haul: A return trip.

back head: The rear elevation of locomotive-boiler mounting controls and instruments.

back-porch yardmaster: The foreman of the yard switchmen.

back pressure: The pressure remaining when a piston exhausts steam against which the steam taken in must work.

back to the farm: Laid off; fired.

bad order: A command placed on a card and tacked to a defective car when examined by the car inspector. The car is not to be moved, except to the *rip track (q.v.)* if the repairs are too extensive to be made on the siding where it stands. The car must be marked with a blue light when men are working on it at night.

baggage: Luggage. A baggage car.

BAGGAGE

　　See baggage, baggage master, baggage room,

baggage smasher, blind baggage, keester keeper, lug, paper car, two-wheeler.

baggage master: The man in charge of the baggage room at a terminal.

baggage room: A room in which baggage, both outgoing and incoming, is kept until shipped or called for.

baggage smasher: A baggage handler.

bail: To fire a locomotive.

bailing-wire artist: An incompetent mechanic, so called from the use the farm mechanic made of the wire from bales of hay; also called *bailing-wire mechanic.*

bail it in: To feed the locomotive firebox.

bake a cake: To get up steam in a locomotive.

bakehead: A fireman.

balanced compound-type engine: A steam locomotive with two high- and two low-pressure cylinders.

baldfacing logs: Loaded log cars being pushed by a locomotive from the rear.

bald wheels: Locomotive drive wheels with the flanges removed to prevent derailment.

ballast: Heavy material such as slag or gravel used to hold crossties in place after rails have been spiked to them. To fill in a track with ballast. Turkey or chicken dressing.

ballast car: An open-top car with sides that swing out and a trap-door bottom for distributing ballast on a roadbed.

ballast scorcher: A speedy engineer.

ballet master: A section boss. See *gandy dancer.*

ball of fire: A fast run. A fast freight train.

balloon: A large sack of mail that expands when thrown from the mail car. A *spark arrester (q.v.).*

balloon stacker: An engine with a balloon-shaped smokestack.

ball the jack: To get speed.

B and B gang: A railroad bridge-and-building crew.

bandwagon: The pay car or pay train from which the wages of the railroad employees are paid.

banjo: A fireman's shovel. A track signal shaped like a banjo.

barefoot: A car or engine without brakes.

barn: A roundhouse for locomotives.

barney: A power car on an incline railroad.

barnhouse: A roundhouse.

barrel: To gain speed. A boiler.

bathe: To take on water at a tank on which the spout is too short or improperly adjusted and douses the fireman with water.

bat out: To switch cars rapidly and expertly.

bat the stack off her: To make fast time. To work an engine at full stroke.

battin' 'em out: An expression used by a switchman when the switch engine is kicking a string of cars all over the yard.

battleship: A large locomotive; also called *battle wagon.* A steel coal car.

battle wagon: See *battleship*.

bazoo wagon: A caboose.

beanery: A railroad eating house.

beanery queen: A waitress.

beans: A lunch period. To meet orders.

bean sheet: The record of a trainman's day's work upon which his wages are based.

bear cat: An unpopular foreman.

bearer: Any small wheel on a truck or attached to an engine frame that supports weight but does not receive power.

bearing: A load-carrying part upon which an axle turns or moves.

bearing block: A metal part bored to receive an axle.

beat her on the back: To get speed or maintain a high rate of speed, using the full power of the engine.

beat the pig: To act as engineer.

beat the throttle with a stick: To get or maintain full speed.

beat the train: To walk the tracks.

bed bug: A Pullman porter.

bed house: A caboose.

beehive: The yardmaster's office. There he gives his orders to the yard foreman or yard conductors.

bell-bottom brakeman: A college student breaking in as a brakeman.

bell ringer: A fireman, so called because it is his duty to ring the bell while the engineer takes care of the whistle signals.

belly of a drag: The underbracings of a railway car.

bend the iron: To throw a switch.

bend the rails: To throw a switch.

bend the rust: To throw a switch.

Berkshire-type engine: A 2-8-4 locomotive introduced in 1925 by the Lima Locomotive Works, Lima, Ohio.

bicycle-type engine: A 4-2-2 locomotive produced by the Baldwin Locomotive Works in 1880.

big boy: A 4-8-8-4 locomotive produced by the American Locomotive Company in the early 1940's for the Union Pacific, said to be the largest ever built. A special train designed for high officials.

big brass: Officials of a railroad company.

big E: An engineer, so called from the large initial on the membership button of the Brotherhood of Locomotive Engineers.

Big Four: The four operating brotherhoods: the Brotherhood of Railway Engineers, the Brotherhood of Railway Firemen, the Brotherhood of Railway Conductors, and the Brotherhood of Railway Trainmen.

big hole: To apply the air-brake valve to make a quick stop in an emergency. The notch on the quadrant of the engineer's brake valve in which the latch of the handle resets during an emergency application of the brakes is larger than the notches used in making graduated-service application. Thus, when the engineer makes an emergency stop, he moves his valve to the *big hole.*

big hook: A huge wrecking crane.

big O: A conductor, so called from the initial on the membership button of the Order of Railway Conductors.

big ox: The freight conductor.

big smoke: A fireman.

binders: A hand brake.

bindle stiff: A hobo who carries a blanket roll. Also called *blanket stiff.*

bird: A twenty-five-cent tip.

bird cage: A brakeman's or switchman's lantern. An observation car. A *spark arrester (q.v.).*

biscuits hang high: A hobo's message to fellow hobos that there is a scarcity of food handouts in the vicinity.

blackball: To blacklist. To boycott.

black diamonds: Company coal.

black hole: A tunnel.

Blackie: A fireman, so called because he was always black with coal dust and smoke.

blackjack: One of the fifty-ton black Santa Fe coal cars.

black one: A railway express car, refrigerator car, or boxcar without interior illumination that has been pressed into mail service during the Christmas rush season.

black snake: A solid train of loaded coal cars.

bladder: The railway postal clerk's name for a newspaper.

blanket stiff: See *bindle stiff.*

blazer: A hot journal box whose packing has caught fire.

bleed: To drain the air from a car or cars.

bleeder: The valve by which air is bled from the *auxiliary reservoir (q.v.)* on a car.

Blenkinsop rack: A third rail with teeth between conventional rails. A running rail with iron pins from its outer surface, used on locomotives with power-driven gear that engages the teeth or pins to prevent slipping.

blind baggage: A baggage car next to the tender. A hobo riding in such a car.

blind gasket: A griddle cake.

blind man: One who rides the *blind baggage (q.v.).* Also called *blind rider.*

blind rider: See *blind baggage.*

blind sag: A soft place under the track that sags as a train passes over it but springs back into place when the train has passed.

blind tires: A locomotive driving wheel with flanges removed to prevent derailment. It adjusts itself to rail curves without binding. Also called *bald wheel.*

blink the headlight: To switch the headlight off and on at an oncoming train to indicate that the blinking train is in the clear on the siding and the switch is aligned for the main line.

blizzard light: In early days, one of two lights placed on either side of the headlight to serve in an emergency when an oil-burning headlight blew out. Later the light indicated that the train was an extra or nonscheduled one. White flags served the same purpose in the daytime. If a regular train was divided into sections, green flags or lights on each train except the last indicated that it was followed within a short interval by another section.

blockhead: A brakeman.

Blood: An old-time engine built by the Manchester Locomotive Works, named after its designer, Aretas Blood.

bloomer-type engine: A 2-2-2 high-wheeler locomotive of the mid-nineteenth century, so called because there were no framing rods outside the driving wheels.

blow her down: To reduce water in a locomotive boiler when it is carrying too much steam. To exhaust steam from the engine, usually in the roundhouse after a run.

blow-in: A person who has just arrived.

blow smoke: To boast. To exaggerate.

blow up: To use the blower to increase draft on the fire and thus raise the steam pressure in the boiler. To quit a job suddenly. To lose one's temper.

blue-tail coat: The dress uniform of a passenger conductor.

B.O.: Short for *bad order*. See *orders*.

board: The blackboard posting the lists of crews in service and their assignments or a list of trains, the hours of departure, and the engine and crews assigned to them. See *call for the board.*

boarding car: A railroad-camp cook shack on wheels.

bobtail: A switch engine.

bobtail bounce: A very short train, usually an engine and a caboose.

bo chaser: Short for *hobo chaser,* a freight brakeman or railroad policeman.

boiled: Drunk.

boiler: A metal tank in which water is converted into steam by heat from the firebox. A locomotive.

boiler ascension: A boiler explosion.

boiler handle: The engine throttle.

boiler head: An engineer.

boiler header: A man riding in the engine cab.

boilermaker: A person who makes, assembles, or repairs boilers. Whisky with a beer chaser.

BOILERMAKER
See boilermaker, hot worker, kettle mender, rivet buster.

boiler wash: A high-water engineer.

boiler water: Whisky.

bolster: A steel beam placed across the frame of a truck to hold the weight of the engine.

bomb: To try to dislodge a hobo from the rods by dropping coal under moving cars so that it would rebound from the ties and strike him. It was not the intention to hurt the tramp, just to give him an uneasy time.

bo money: A bribe paid to a brakeman by a hobo for a ride, usually a dollar a division.

boneyard: The repair tracks. The end of the line for worn-out rolling stock.

boob: A railroad tie cutter.

bookkeeper: A flagman.

book-of-rules: An examination based upon such facts as are found in the rule book.

boomer: A railroad worker who changed jobs often as he drifted through the country. He was not really a tramp but was of that breed who could not be tied down to one location long, though he had no trouble getting a job during the rush season because of his experience and knowledge of railroading.

booster: An extra engine used to help pull or push a train over a steep hill or mountain.

bootlegger: A train that runs over more than one railroad.

bo park: A railroad yard frequented by hoboes; also called *bo yard*.

bore: The inner diameter of a cylinder or cylinder cavity.

boss: A conductor, so called because he has charge of the train.

boss's eye: A railway detective.

Boston quarter: A nickel or dime tip.

bouncer: A caboose, especially one of the little early-day four-wheelers.

bowling alley: A hand-fired locomotive, so called because of the manner in which the fireman threw coal, using the motions of bowling.

box: Short for *boxcar*.

boxcar: A roofed freight car with sliding doors in the sides.

boxcar artist: A tramp who steals rides on the train.

boxer: A boxcar.

boxcar tourist: A hobo riding the rods.

boy: The porter on a passenger train.

bo yard: A railway yard frequented by tramps; also called *bo park*.

brain box: A private car. A caboose.

brain cage: A caboose, so called because the conductor rides in it.

brainless wonder: Anyone—conductor, engineer, fireman, or other—who does odd things.

brain plate: A trainman's badge attached to his hat or cap.

brains: A conductor. A trainmaster. A train dispatcher.

brain wagon: A caboose.

BRAKE

See air, air-brake instruction car, air-brake repair car, air-brake tests, air monkey, air pipe, anchors, barefoot, big hole, binders, brake club, brake cylinder, brake hose, brake pipe, brake shoe, go high, goose, pull the air, put it in the big hole, shoot the works, throw her into the big hole, tie the train down, whiz, wipe the gauge.

brake club: A hard, three-foot club used by freight brakemen to tighten hand brakes. It was a standard part of their equipment. During the old link-and-pin days it was handy in prying up coupling pins to loosen them and was also a protection against an ill-tempered tramp.

brake cylinder: An iron cylinder containing a piston operated by compressed air to apply air brakes.

brake hickey: An iron bar with a hook. It was thrust between the spokes of the brake wheel and hooked over the shaft to provide added leverage in applying the brakes.

brake hose: A flexible tube used to connect brake pipes between cars.

brakeman: One who brakes a train. One who operates or repairs brakes. In early days he was the lowest-paid crewman. His job was climbing on tops of cars and jumping on or off moving trains. He had to run ahead of an engine, throw a switch, and stand there until the train had passed. He had to work in the rain, snow, and sleet. If he was a rear brakeman, he had to go back some distance behind the train and flag, or *torpedo (q.v.)*, a following train, no matter how bad the weather.

BRAKEMAN

See air giver, baby lifter, bakehead, bell, bell-bottom brakeman, brakeman, car catcher, car hand, clown, club winder, cook, donnigan, dude wrangler, end man, fielder, fixed man, fixed signal, flag, fourth man, front shack, ground hog, head brakeman, head man, head pin, head shack, hink hook, hind shack, hose coupler, hump brakie, iron bender, juggler, middle man, middle swing, mule, nearsighted shack, nipper, parlor brakeman, parlor man, pin, pin head, pin lifter, pin puller, rear shack, ride the smoky end, roughneck, scissorbill, shack, shack stinger, shag, smoke, smoke agent, staff of ignorance, stargazer, stringer, student smoke agent, student tallow pot, swing brakeman, swing man, tar pot, thin skin, trailer man, wheelman.

brake partners with: To work with another brakeman.

brake pipe: An iron pipe connecting the engineer's brake valve to the air-brake mechanism on the cars behind.

braker: A brakeman. Also called *brakie.*

brake shoe: A crescent-shaped piece of metal that drags against the tread of a wheel when the brake is applied.

brakie: See *braker.*

brass: A babbitt-lined piece of bronze that forms a bearing upon which a railroad car rests. One is *brassing* a car when replacing such a bearing, which is easily done by jacking up the journal box to remove the brass. This was often done on the road when there was a *hotbox (q.v.).*

brass: The locomotive bell. High officials.

brass buttons: A passenger-train conductor.

brass collar: Officialdom, usually those above division officials.

brass hat: A rail official or executive.

brass pounder: A telegraph operator, so called because his sending instruments are made of brass.

brat the pig: To act as engineer.

break in two: To break apart; said of a train that separated while in motion in the early days of link-and-pin couplers.

brick arch: A sloping barrier made of firebrick in the engine furnace to hold the fire and embers before they reached the flues. The idea for the arch was originated in 1857, but it did not become popular until 1900.

bridge hog: A bridge carpenter of the old school, before the days of steel and concrete.

bridge monkey: A bridge builder; also called *bridge stiff*.

bridge stiff: See *bridge monkey*.

bridge wall: A water-filled partition partly separating a forward extension of the furnace from the coal-burning section.

broad gauge: A railroad gauge wider than the standard gauge, 4 feet, 8½ inches; also called *broad-gauge line*.

broken knuckles: An expression describing railroad sleeping quarters.

broken rail: An old hand at railroading.

brownie: A demerit. In 1885, George R. Brown decided that suspending a worker for breaking a rule was unfair to the family, and he conceived the idea of substituting a system of demerits. If a worker received too many demerits and persisted in breaking the rules, he was fired. This system was soon adopted by all railroads.

brownie box: The railroad superintendent's private car.

brownie buster: A boxcar burglar.

brownie can: The can in which a flagman carried signal torpedoes.

brownie wagon: A *brownie box (q.v.)*.

bub: To stop. To correct an error.

bucket: The piston on a diesel electric engine.

bucket plow: An extraheavy snow plow used when the snow is too heavy for the ordinary plow. It is used as a battering ram pushed by several locomotives, which back up and hit the packed snow on the fly.

buck the board: To be without a regular run. To work any run the terminal foreman assigns. If, on the extra board, the worker is called only when there is more work than the regular crew can handle, then he takes his turn.

buck the snow: To run an engine, usually with a snow plow, to push an accumulation of snow from the track.

buda car: An inspection car with an automobile-type body and flanged wheels driven by a 100-horsepower engine.

bug: The sending instrument of the telegrapher. Many operators carried their own private bugs. A flashlight lantern.

buggy: A caboose, so called because of its semielliptic springs instead of the coil springs used on freight cars.

buggy track: A track in the yards upon which a caboose is kept when not in use.

bug line: The telephone line between the engine house and the yard or telegraph office.

bug slinger: A switchman or brakeman, so called for his lighted lantern.

bug torch: A flashlight lantern.

bull: A locomotive. A special agent. A railroad policeman who checks on the activities of all railroad employees as well as those of trespassers.

bulletin board: A six-sided board mounted on a pivot. By rotating it, one could read the new job assignments.

bulletined: Listed on the bulletin board; one's name was placed on the board after his cycle of duty to alert anyone else interested in an assignment through his seniority.

bullfighter: An empty car, especially a passenger car.

bullgine: A steam locomotive.

bull goose: The yardmaster.

bullnose: The front drawbar of a locomotive.

bull pen: The crew room at a terminal.

bump: To demote. To take the turn of another railroader. When bidding on a vacancy, the man with the most seniority and longest record of service received the job.

bump a run: To take another man's run.

bumper: A retaining post at the end of a spur track, a device for absorbing shock and preventing damage in a collision.

bum-sick train: A train run by a crew hostile to tramps.

bunch of thieves: A wrecking crew.

bunk car: A sleeping car for loggers or track workers.

bunkhouse: A freight car filled with bunks, such as those used by a section gang.

Bury firebox: A furnace invented by Edward Bury in the early 1830's. It was popular until the introduction of larger engines, which required larger grate areas.

bus: A locomotive.

bust a brownie: To rob a boxcar.

bust head: Whisky.

bust up a cut: To separate cars in a train, removing those that have reached their destination and switching others to through trains.

butch: A boy or man peddling candy, fruits, and magazines on passenger trains. Also called *candy butcher, news butch.*

butter-and-egg run: The run of a local passenger train.

butterfly: A note from a trainman thrown to a section employee, so called because of its fluttering motion along the track.

buzzard's roost: The yard office.

buzzer: A telegraph operator.

C

cab: The section of the locomotive that houses the engineer, the fireman, and the operating controls. It came into being in 1843.

cabbage cutter: A freight engine, so called because its main and side rods swept close to the ground at its lowest points.

cabbage stack: An early-day locomotive smokestack that was shaped like a large cabbagehead. The bulbous top served as a repository for the wood ashes. The stacks were used only during the days of the woodburner engines.

cabin car: A caboose.

caboose: A freight-train car attached to the rear of the train for the use of the crew. There the conductor takes care of his papers and orders, and the rear brakeman rides in it to protect the rear of the train. It is also there that the trainmen prepare their meals and stockmen ride when traveling with a shipment of cattle. On short runs it was once often used to carry passengers.

CABOOSE
    See anchor, angel's seat, animal car, ape wag-

on, bazoo wagon, bed house, bouncer, brain cage, brain wagon, buggy, buggy track, cabin car, caboose, caboose bounce, caboose hop, cage, chariot, chuck wagon, clown wagon, cook loft, conductor's car, cook shack, coop, cracker box, crib, cripple's home, crow's nest, crumb box, crummy, cupola, den, doghouse, doodlebug, doss, drawing room, flophouse, flop wagon, galloping goose, glory wagon, go-cart, hack, hay wagon, hearse, hut, kipps, kitchen, library, louse cage, monitor, monkey cage, monkey house, monkey hut, monkey wagon, palace, parlor, parlor end, pavilion, penthouse, perambulator, possum belly, rest room, saloon, shack, shack house, shanty, shelter house, strawberry patch, skunk speeder, sun parlor, top dresser drawer, treasure chest, van, way car, zoo.

caboose bounce: An early train composed of only an engine and a caboose. Also called *caboose hop*.

caboose hop: See *caboose bounce*.

caboose track fry: Sliced potatoes and onions fried in deep grease as cooked in the caboose.

cad: A conductor. A baggageman.

cage: A caboose.

cage full of signals: A signal lantern.

call book: A book carried by the *call boy (q.v.)* to be signed by the men called to duty. The book resolved many disagreements and relieved the call boy of blame because it held a record of whether or not the one called had signed.

call boy: A boy whose duty it was to summon train

and engine crews for regular runs or extra trains. He knew where most of the trainmen hung out and rode his bicycle to summon them and get their signature in his greasy *call book (q.v.)*.

CALL BOY

See call book, call boy, caller, punk, skunk, speedy, zookeeper.

caller: A *call boy (q.v.)*. The train announcer at a station.

call for the board: To sound the whistle for a semaphore signal when approaching a station. The signal told the engineer whether to stop or to proceed and whether he had orders. If he had orders, they were attached to a hoop and passed to the trainman by an agent.

calliope: A steam locomotive, so called because of its four-tone whistles.

camelback: A locomotive with the cab on top of the boiler, suggesting the hump of a camel. Also called *Mother Hubbard*.

camel-type engine: An 0-8-0 engine having the appearance of a dromedary owing to the placement of the steam dome and controls in front of the furnace.

camp car: In logging, a building on railroad trucks used for sleeping, cooking, office, and other purposes.

cam-set watch: A railroad watch on which the hands are set by a release lever instead of by the spindle alone.

can: A tank car.

canal: To run a train leisurely.

candy butcher: A *butch (q.v.);* see also *news butch.*

candy run: A short, easy haul.

candy train: A train transporting jewelry.

canned: Discharged. Drunk.

cannonball express: A fast train.

captain: A freight- or passenger-train conductor.

car catcher: A rear brakeman.

card: Credentials showing membership in a union or brotherhood.

car frog: A heavy piece of steel spiked to a tie and used to get a derailed wheel back on the rails.

car hand: A brakeman.

car handle: A drawbar.

carhouse car: A covered cement car.

car inspector: One who inspects railroad cars for defects and needed repairs.

CAR INSPECTOR
See car knocker, car inspector, car tink, car toad, car tonk, car whacker, dope monkey, galvanizer, hot-box dick, master car repairer, wheel monkey.

car knocker: A car inspector or car repairman, so called from his custom of tapping the wheels of a car to discover flaws. Also called *car tink, car toad, car tonk, car whacker.*

car line: A line used to pull railroad cars into position for loading.

carload: A load that fills a car. A minimum number

of tons required for shipping at carload rates.

carry a flag: To travel off schedule. To run a train in sections.

carry green: To display green flags on a train by day and green lights by night to show that a second train is closely following.

carry the banner: To display flags. To wear brotherhood emblems as hobos frequently did when trying for a handout.

carry the mail: To bring train orders. To get speed.

carry the white feather: An expression describing a plume of steam showing above the safety valve of the engine.

carry white: To fly white streamers to indicate that the train is a special or nonscheduled train.

caser: A silver dollar.

Casey: A new employee.

Casey Jones: A locomotive engineer, especially a fast-running one. The name is derived from John Luther ("Casey") Jones, a noted engineer on a southern railroad whose death in a wreck became a legend.

caterpillar: A streamlined passenger train.

catter: One who clings to the outside of cars, especially on a *blind baggage (q.v.).*

cattle car: A stock car.

cattle guard: A steel sheet with closely spaced triangular pieces projected above the sheet and spiked to the ties between the rails, placed at road crossings where cattle are likely to enter the fenced right of way.

catwalk: A narrow platform on the locomotive. A running board on top of a boxcar used by brakemen to go from one car to another to set hand brakes.

century: A one-hundred-dollar bill.

chain gang: A regular crew assigned special duties. When a number of extra trains are being run, regular crews may be assigned to trains in turns rather than to specific scheduled runs. A section gang.

chair: A steel clamp supporting a rail.

chair car: A passenger car with pairs of chairs on each side of the aisle with individually adjustable backs.

Challenger-type engine: A high-speed 4-6-6-4 articulated engine used in either passenger or freight service.

chambermaid: A roundhouse machinist.

charge the train line: To fill the air-brake reservoirs on each car. The expression means that the steam pressure is on the 200-pound mark.

chariot: A caboose. The general manager's car.

chase the red: To show a red flag or lantern to protect a train.

checker: A company spy, especially one checking on the loss of materials or the receipts of an agent or conductor.

checkerboard crew: A mixed crew of white and black track workers.

cherry picker: A switchman, so called because of the red lights on the switch stands. A man who is choosy about jobs and passes up those he does not want. A mounted crane used to lift heavy equipment.

Chesapeake-type engine: A 2-8-8-2 articulated locomotive first used on the Chesapeake & Ohio Railroad; a good engine for pulling steep grades and heavy loads.

chew cinders: Said of an engine that is reversed while running or working a lot of steam.

chief clerk: The man who takes care of the office work, such as correspondence, reports, and accounts.

chilled rim: The circumference of a cast-iron wheel toughened by a special process in which an iron mold is used rather than one of sand. When the melted iron comes in contact with such a mold, it quickly solidifies and produces hard-wearing treads and flanges.

chippy: A narrow-gauge car.

chisel: To switch cars in the switch yard.

chuck wagon: A caboose.

cinder: A partly burned piece of coal capable of further burning without flame. In the old days, when unscreened windows were left open for air, cinders caused some discomfort to passengers, such as cinder dust in the eyes or burned holes in clothing. The railroad right of way, an expression used by hobos. Also called *cinder trail*.

cinder bull: A railway detective.

cinder cruncher: A switchman or flagman.

cinder dick: A railroad policeman or detective.

cinder grifter: A hobo who walks the track.

cinder pit: A pit near the roundhouse. Built of concrete and filled with water, it was used by the engineers as a dump for their cinder pan before they drove their engines into the roundhouse. Later the cinders were used for surfacing tracks, filling washouts, and making other repairs.

cinder sifter: A tramp who walks along the track.

cinder snapper: A passenger riding on an observation platform.

cinder trail: See *cinder.*

circus: The railroad.

City of Iron Horses: Paterson, New Jersey, so called because many locomotives were manufactured there.

claw: A clinker hook used by firemen.

claw bar: A heavy steel bar with a turned-up claw at the lower end, used for pulling track spikes.

clean the clock: To make an emergency stop. In such an emergency all pressure is removed so that the clocklike gauge shows zero.

clearance card: The authority to use the main line.

clear board: A go-ahead signal.

CLERK
 See mud hop, number dummy, nut buster, paperweight, pencil pusher, shiny pants.

clinker: A mass of hot coals fused together.

clip: A note or short message.

clock: A steam gauge. A fare register.

close the gate: To close a switch.

clover picker: A cowboy accompanying a shipment of cattle.

clown: A switchman or yard brakeman.

clown wagon: A caboose.

club: See *brake club*.

club car: A lounge car; a passenger car with seats for lounging and facilities for serving refreshments.

club 'em down: To set hand brakes with the aid of a brake club.

club winder: A switchman or brakeman.

COAL

> *See* asbestos, black diamonds, idiot stick, dirt, lampblack, lump oil, nuts, real estate, rock, slack, tool of ignorance.

coal chute: A place where coal for the engine was stored.

coaler: A railway that transports much coal. A coal-burning locomotive. A coal car.

coal eight: A coal car.

coal heaver: A fireman; also called *stoker*.

coal road: A railway that hauls much coal.

coaly: A fireman.

cobs: Coal.

cock-eyed: Drunk.

cock loft: The cupola of a caboose.

coffee: A rest period taken while baggagemen are waiting for the next train.

coffeepot: An old, small steam locomotive.

coffin varnish: Whisky.

collar-and-elbow joint: A boardinghouse, so called because there is never much room at the table.

color blind: Light-fingered; said of an employee who could not distinguish his money from the company's.

Columbia-type engine: A 2-4-2 locomotive, first produced by Baldwin in 1892.

combination train: A mixed freight and local passenger train.

combustion chamber: A space in the engine boiler where combustion is promoted and additional heat obtained from the gases before they enter the fire tubes.

come along: A hand signal meaning to come ahead.

comet: One who rides passenger trains.

commutation ticket: A ticket sold at reduced rate for a fixed number of trips over the same route during a limited period.

commuter: A passenger who travels back and forth regularly over the same line.

company bible: The company book of rules.

company jewelry: A trainman's switch keys, badge, and cap.

company notch: The point of the locomotive throttle

that gives the most pulling power—the forward corner of the reverse rear quadrant.

compound-type engine: A steam locomotive using steam released from one cylinder in a second cylinder.

con: Short for *conductor.*

conducer: A conductor.

CONDUCTOR

See big O, big ox, boiler head, boiler wash, boss, brainless wonder, brains, brass buttons, cad, captain, conducer, conductor, con, conny, crum boss, cushion rider, dinger, drum, drummer, ducat, dud, gold buttons, grabber [passenger], hot-footer, king [freight], king pin, master, master mind, old man, ORC, pair of pliers, ride the cushions, ride the plush, ride the velvet, shack's master, silk gloves, skin your eye, skipper, smart alec, swellhead, ticket snatcher [passenger], wear brass buttons.

conductor's car: A caboose.

connecting rod: A large rectangular steel rod that transmits the motion of the piston and piston rod to the driving wheels of the engine.

conny: Short for *conductor.*

consist: A report sent ahead by the conductor to the yardmaster at the next stop to allow him to plan switchings. It is sent to the operator and gives the makeup of the train, car types, the freight's destination, and other information.

consolidation-type engine: A locomotive of the 2-8-0

wheel arrangement designed in 1865 and used in freight service.

construction train: A work train used in railroad construction.

cook: A rear brakeman.

cook shack: A caboose, so called because the trainmen's meals are often prepared in it.

cool a spindle: To cool a hotbox by replacing the brass or putting water on the bearings.

coon: To move across the tops of cars of a freight train. To run a train at reduced speed. Also *coon a train, coon it.*

cornered: Said of a car struck by an engine or train because it is not in the clear on a siding.

cornfield meet: A head-on collision, or one narrowly averted.

couldn't pull a settin' hen off the nest: Said of an old-fashioned locomotive whose pulling power is weak.

count the ties: To reduce speed. To walk the track. To quit a job. To be fired.

COUPLE CARS
> *See* hitch, hook up, tie one, tie 'em together, pick up.

coupler: A mechanism for fastening together individual cars and the engine of a train.

cow cage: A stock car.

cowcatcher: A device made of outthrust wrought-iron bars placed in front of the engine to push cattle aside. Before its invention (by Isaac Dripps) many trains were wrecked running over cattle because there was nothing to prevent them from falling under the engine.

cow crate: A stock car.

cow wagon: A dining car.

crab-type engine: A locomotive whose main and side rods are stroked in opposite directions, similar to the motion of a crab.

cracker box: A caboose.

crack the black diamonds: To work as a fireman.

crack the throttle: To open the throttle easy. To start an engine slowly.

crack train: A superior train.

crack-up: A wreck.

cradle: A gondola or other open-top car.

Crampton-type engine: A locomotive with a single pair of driving wheels about eight feet in diameter. The wheels had poor traction because of inadequate weight.

crank axle: A driving axle with cranks within the wheels mounted upon it to which the main rods furnish motion.

crank disk: One of two flat iron pieces attached to the driving axle, fastened with a crank pin. Also called *crank web*.

crank pin: A short piece attached to a crank on a driving wheel of the crank axle.

crank web: See *crank disk*.

crate: A boxcar.

crawler: A dragline bucket used to move dirt on a right of way.

crew car: In logging, any car used to carry the crew to work in the woods.

crew dispatcher: A specialist who assigns crews to trains.

crib: A caboose.

cripple: A car in bad condition.

cripple's home: A caboose.

croaker: A company doctor.

croppy: A train of perishable freight that has spoiled in transit.

cross-compound-type engine: A locomotive with a high-pressure cylinder on one side and a low-pressure cylinder on the other, the latter using the exhaust steam of the first.

crossing watchman: A safety watchman at a point where two railroads cross. He usually spends his time between trains in a little shack.

crosstie: A wooden tie placed at right angles to and beneath the rails to support them.

crown: To couple a caboose to a freight train, an operation which, together with a proper display of markers, differentiates a train from a *cut of cars (q.v.).*

crown him: To couple a caboose to a freight train after it has been made up.

crown sheet: The roof of a firebox. A flapjack, so called because the bubble holes are similar to those in a locomotive crown sheet.

crow's nest: The cupola of a caboose.

crumb boss: The man in charge of *camp cars (q.v.).*

crumb box: A caboose.

crumb bundle: A tramp's possessions tied up in a bandanna.

crummy: A caboose.

culm: The screening of refuse coal.

cupola: The observation tower of a caboose. From that vantage point it was possible for the brakeman to spot hot journals, brake beams that had dropped down, and other dangers.

CUPOLA
> *See* angel's seat, crow's nest, cock loft, cupola, cupola waver, penthouse.

cupola waver: A freight trainman who sits in the cupola of the caboose and waves at the girls as his train passes.

cushions: A passenger car.

cushion rider: A passenger-train conductor. A member of a passenger-train crew. A passenger.

cut of cars: Several cars attached to an engine, or coupled together by themselves. A right of way that has been excavated across a mountain rather than run over it or tunneled through it.

cutout cock: A valve located below the brake valve; when it is set, it is impossible to move the train.

cut the board: To lay off the most recently hired man on the extra list. To reduce crews.

cut the buck: To build steam to full working pressure.

cut the train line: To connect the air-brake hose between the engine and the cars.

cylinder: A chamber through which a piston is driven.

cylinder head: The metal cover on the end of a cylinder.

daisy-chain: Said when cars pull off the track on sharp curves.

dance on the carpet: To be called to the office for discipline or an investigation.

dangler: A freight train. One who rides the rods.

day coach: An inexpensive passenger coach.

dead engine: An engine being hauled or pushed.

deadhead: An employee riding on a pass. A nonpaying passenger. The head brakeman, who rides in the engine cab. Unused empty cars on a train being sent to another point.

dead iron, live iron: The two sets of tracks on a scale.

deadline: The end of the line for rolling stock.

deadman: A tree or secure post to which blocks are fastened in wrecking operations.

deadman's button: See *deadman's throttle.*

deadman's control: See *deadman's throttle.*

deadman's hole: A method of righting an overturned engine or car. Some distance from the overturned vehicle a hole is dug long enough to hold a large plank. A trench is dug to the vehicle, and heavy ropes are placed in it. To the underside of the overturned vehicle are fastened chains, which are then fastened to the drawbar of the road engine. To hold the deadman down against the pull, the hole is filled and packed hard. The road engine then moves up the track, pulling the ropes over the top of the vehicle on the chains fastened to the lower part and thus rolling the wrecked vehicle onto its wheels.

deadman's throttle: A throttle that requires the pressure of the operator's hand to maintain power and to prevent the application of brakes. An engine so equipped would stop if the engineer suddenly died and the throttle pressure ceased. Also called *deadman's control.*

death woods: Narrow strips of wood on the ends of boxcars above the couplings, providing uncertain footing.

decapod-type engine: A freight locomotive with a 2-10-0 wheel arrangement, introduced in 1867.

deck: The front part of the engine cab. The catwalk on top of boxcars.

deck hand: One who rides the roofs of freight cars.

deck kitchen: The floor of the locomotive cab.

decorate: To set hand brakes. To receive or transmit signals. To climb on top of freight cars.

dehorned: To be demoted or discharged.

delayer: A train dispatcher.

den: A caboose.

depot: A railway station.

detainer: A train dispatcher.

DETECTIVE
> *See* bo chaser, boss's eye, bull, checker, cinder bull, cinder dick, dick, egg, eye, gumshoe, nighthawk, plant, pussyfooter, rail, rat, red light, silent eye, spotter, tin star, train bull, train dick, undercover man, yard bull, yard dick.

dewdrop: To try to dislodge a tramp from the rods by dropping chunks of coal under moving cars with the hope that they will rebound from the ties and frighten the tramp.

diamond: A railroad crossover.

diamond cracker: A fireman on a coal-burning locomotive; also called *diamond heaver, diamond pusher, diamond thrower.*

diamonds: Coal.

diamond stack: A locomotive with a diamond-shaped *spark arrester (q.v.)* on the smoke stack.

diamond thrower: See *diamond cracker.*

dicer: A fast freight train.

dick: A railroad detective.

die: To stall on a hill.

die game: The stalling of a train on a hill.

diesel engine: An internal-combustion engine in which compressed air is used to fire the fuel injected into the cylinders.

dilly road: A railroad track in a mine.

diner: A dining car on a passenger train. Poor food

was served at high prices, which did not endear the railroads to the traveler.

ding-dong: A gas coach that ran on short branch roads that could not support regular trains, so called because of the sound of its bell.

dinger: A conductor. A yardmaster or his assistant.

dinky: A switch engine with a tender, used around the shops and roundhouse.

dinky skinner: A logging-train engineer.

diploma: A clearance or service letter. A fake service letter.

dirt: Fine coal.

dirt dauber: A road grader; also called *dirt hider*.

dirt track: A roadbed without ballast under the ties. Such tracks could be used only in dry weather by trains with light loads.

dirty car: A storage car containing various kinds of parcels and mail that required extra work to sort.

dispatcher: One of the most important employees in railroading. He controls the movement of all trains, and therefore his office never closes. He has to know where each train is, where trains are to meet, and how much time one or the other has lost.

DISPATCHER
  See delayer, detainer, dispatcher, greetings from the DS, moving spirit, OS, OS-ing, train dispatcher.

dishwasher: An engine wiper at a roundhouse.

ditch: That part of a right of way lower than the

roadbed. To throw a tramp off a train. To cause a wreck. To cause a train to derail.

division: One of a number of sections of a railroad separated by terminals, usually a hundred miles apart, where train and engine crews change.

division jump: A long-distance train ride, from one division to another; also called *division leap.*

division leap: See *division jump.*

division point: One of many sections of a railroad, independent of the other divisions and having its own crews, officials, locomotives, and shops.

dog catcher: A member of a crew sent to relieve another crew that had been outlawed—that is, overtaken on the road by the sixteen-hour law, which prohibited the first crew from moving it. Also called *dog chaser, dog law.*

doghouse: A caboose. The cupola of a caboose. In logging railroading, a cabin placed on the tender of the locomotive for the conductor's use.

dog law: See *dog catcher.*

dog leg: A sharp reverse curve in the track.

dolly: A switch stand.

dolly flapper: A switch tender.

Dolly Varden: The buffer on an old-style tender, named for Dickens' flirtatious heroine of *Barnaby Rudge.*

Donegan: An old car from which the wheels have been removed, used as an office or a residence.

donkey: A small auxiliary engine. A section man.

donniker: A freight brakeman. A privy.

do not order: In the early days, an important order not to pass a certain station without further orders.

doodlebug: A rail motor car used by linemen, section hands, and others; also called *ding-dong*. A caboose.

door slammer: A brakeman. In the early days of railroading the wooden passenger cars were flimsy, and the rough track caused strains that made it hard to open and close doors. It was the slamming of the doors by the brakeman that gave him this name.

dope: An order or official instructions. A heavy, black semiliquid cooling compound for hot journals.

dope bucket: A container for *dope (q.v.).*

dope it: To use *dope (q.v.)* in the water to keep it from boiling when working an engine hard.

dope monkey: A car inspector who sees that there is *dope (q.v.)* in the journals.

dope puller: One who pulls lubricating waste out of journal boxes.

doss: A caboose.

double: In pulling a hill, to cut the train in half and take each section up separately.

double-acting engine: An engine in which steam is directed alternately into the two ends of a closed cylinder, doing away with the unpowered return stroke of the piston.

double-decked stock: A stock car with two floors, used for hauling sheep.

double-ender: A locomotive built to run either direction. It has twin boilers with a central cab and firebox and a trucklike cylinder and driving-wheel assembly beneath each barrel.

double-gun: To work both injectors at one. See *injector.*

double the hill: See *double.*

doubleheader: A train hauled by two engines, especially in mountains and during heavy snows.

double in: To bring cars from a siding onto the main track and attach them behind a car left on the main track.

douse the glim: To extinguish a lantern, especially with a sudden upward movement.

down the cinders: Along the railroad track.

drag: A slow train, as contrasted to a *hotshot (q.v.).* A long, slow train trip. To haul a train of dead freight.

drag belly: The underbracings of a railway car.

drawbar: A *coupler (q.v.).*

drawbar flagging: Said of a flagman who, in protecting the rear of his train, is supposed to go back some distance behind his train but, for fear of getting left behind, leans against the drawbar of the caboose to give his signal.

draw head: The frame through which a drawbar is attached to a railroad car.

drawing room: A caboose.

drift: To operate a locomotive on a downgrade without working steam.

drift throttle: To run a locomotive with the steam

throttle open to keep air and dust from being sucked into the steam cylinders.

drill: A switch engine. A switch-engine crew.

drill crew: A yard crew.

drink: Water for the locomotive. To take on water.

driving axle: The axle on which the driving wheels of a locomotive are mounted.

driving box: A housing containing the bearing for the *driving axle (q.v.).*

driving unit: An assembly of cylinders, rods, driving wheels, valve gear, and brakes attached to an engine bed.

driving wheel: One of the wheels of the locomotive connected to the main or side rods to transform power to traction.

driver: One of the large main wheels of a locomotive. A leg; the trainman sometimes called his legs *drivers.*

drone cage: A private car.

drop: A switching movement in which cars are cut off from the engine and allowed to coast to the desired spot.

drop a car: To switch a car with a *flying switch (q.v.).*

drop a little run-fast: To oil the engine.

drop her bundle: To run out of steam.

drop her in the corner: To drop the *Johnson bar (q.v.)* in one corner of the cab to make fast time.

drop her down: To pull the reverse lever forward.

dropper: A switchman riding a car on the *hump (q.v.).*

drop the consist: To drop the *consist (q.v.)* off a moving train to the operator or station agent.

drop the sand: To open the valve that releases sand from the *sand dome (q.v.)* to the track in front of the drivers.

drown it out: To cool an overheated journal.

drum: A hard-shelled conductor. A switching of cars in a switchyard.

drummer: A yard conductor.

DRUNK
> *See* boiled, canned, cock-eyed, frazzled, fried, oiled, ossified, pifflicated, pie-eyed, plastered, snozzled, stewed.

drunkard: A late Saturday night passenger train. The last commuting train from a city terminal.

ducat: A passenger conductor's hat check. A ticket.

duckboard: The platform running along the top of a boxcar.

dude: A passenger conductor.

dude train: A train on which extra fares are charged.

dude wrangler: A passenger-train brakeman.

dummy: Short for *dummy locomotive*, a type of switch engine on which the boiler and running gear are housed. A train for employees. A car running on its own power.

dump the air: To uncover all the openings in the control valves of an air-brake system at once in an emergency so that the brake's full force can be applied.

dump the pan: To discard the action of the engine

crew while emptying the fire and clinkers from the locomotive's ash pan.

duplex air compressor: An air compressor containing two steam cylinders and two compound air cylinders that deliver air and pressure to the main reservoir.

dust: To feed sand through the flues of an oil burner to cut the soot deposit.

duster: A locomotive.

dust her out: To put sand through the firebox of an oil burner while working the engine hard to cut the soot from the flues.

dust raiser: A fireman who is shoveling coal into the firebox.

Dutch clock: A speed recorder installed by the company to see that freight trains did not exceed eighteen miles per hour. Trainmen did not like this slow pace and found a way to jimmy the clock by uncoupling the caboose, where the clock was located, and letting it slam into the train at a speed of eighteen miles per hour. After that the clock would register that speed no matter how fast the train moved.

Dutch drop: A rarely used method of switching to bring a car onto the main line from a spur. This was done by heading the engine onto the spur, coupling head on to the car, and then backing out. After reaching the proper speed, the engine was cut away and then speeded to get back onto the main line ahead of the car, then moved forward ahead of the car and ahead of the junction between the main line and the spur so that the car would roll out behind the engine.

Dutchman: A short piece of rail used to fill in at places where the longer rail had worn out.

dynamiter: A car having some defective mechanism that sends the brakes into an emergency when only a *service application (q.v.)* has been applied by the engineer.

dynamite her: To stop a train suddenly.

eagle eye: A locomotive engineer, so called because he must constantly be on the lookout for signals and obstacles.

easy sign: A signal indicating that the train is to move slowly.

eccentric: A circular steel plate having a hole slightly off center, mounted on a driving axle. It is used on a locomotive to actuate the valve-gear mechanism controlling the forward and backward motion.

egg: A railroad policeman.

eight-wheeler: A large locomotive with eight drive wheels.

ejector: A device for exhausting air in a vacuum brake.

electric owl: A night operator.

elephant car: A special car coupled behind the locomotive to accommodate the head brakeman.

em: One thousand pounds of tonnage.

emigrant ticket: A transportation ticket sold to an emigrant at reduced prices.

emigrant train: A train carrying emigrants such as those of the early days when families were seeking homes in the West.

end man: The rear brakeman on a freight train.

engine: A railroad locomotive.

ENGINE

See Allegheny-type engine, American-type engine, articulated engine, Atlantic-type engine, battleship, Berkshire-type engine, bicycle-type engine, bloomer-type engine, bobtail, boiler, camelback-type engine, camel-type engine, Challenger-type engine, Chesapeake-type engine, coaler, Columbia-type engine, compound-type engine, consolidated-type engine, Crampton-type engine, cross-compound-type engine, dead engine, dead head, decapod-type engine, diesel engine, dinky, double-acting engine, double-ender, drill, dummy, fantail, goat, grasshopper-type engine, hay burner, helper, high-pressure engine, high-wheeler, Hudson-type engine, Killingsworth-type engine, light engine, little Nemo, low-pressure engine, Mallet, mastodon-type engine, mighty Mogul, Mikado-type engine, Mike, mogul, Mother hubbard, mountain-type engine, mud digger, mudscow, oiler, Pacific-type engine, prairie-type engine, pusher, quadruplex-type engine, quintuplex-type engine, rammer, sacred cow, sacred ox, Samson-class engine, Shay-type engine, sidewinder, shunting boiler, tallow pit, tandem compound-type engine, tank engine, tank-type engine, Texas-type engine, three-cylinder compound-type engine, tramp, triplex-type engine, Vauclain compound-type engine, Whyte classification, Yellowstone-type engine.

engine bed: The underframe assembly of a locomotive.

engineer: A man trained to run a locomotive.

ENGINEER

See air artist, ballet scorcher, beat the pig, big E, boiler head, boiler wash, booster, brainless wonder, brat the pig, Casey Jones, driver, eagle eye, engineer, engine rapper, engine tamer, engine trimmer, fast roller, grunt, hog eye, hogger, hogineer, hog head, hog jerker, hog jockey, hog master, hog mauler, hog-footer, hot-rodder, lockey man, lung doctor, lung specialist, mileage hog, paddle the boiler, pig mauler, pig skinner, plug puller, positive block, pounder, rapper, rawhider, right-hand side, runner, skin your eye, speed gauger, stack buster, swellhead, throttle puller, traveling man, two-gun hogger, underdog, underground hog, whistle pig, work water, young runner.

engine rapper: An engineer who fails to *hook 'er up and pull 'er tail (q.v.);* also called *engine trimmer.*

engine tamer: An engineer who breaks in a new locomotive.

engine trimmer: See *engine rapper.*

equalizer: A beam connecting two axle springs to distribute the weight of a locomotive equally.

Espee: The Southern Pacific Railroad.

express car: A car on a passenger train in which items are shipped by the express company.

express man: A man who handles the express shipments.

express office: Usually the downtown office of the express company.

extra: A train not listed on the timetable.

extra board: A list of men, usually seven or eight, who are available for new assignments, such as on extras, doubleheaders, or work trains or as replacements for men on the sick list.

extra gang: A section gang put on extra duty because of a wreck, a flood, or a suddenly discovered defect in the track or roadbed.

eye: A trackside signal. A railroad detective.

Fairlie-type engine: An 0-4-4-0 double-ended locomotive invented in 1866. It was unsatisfactory and short-lived.

Fairlie-Mason-type engine: An 0-6-6-0 double-ended locomotive introduced in 1871. Because of the difficulty of carrying enough fuel, its use was discontinued in 1877.

fake head: A fireman.

falling-off place: A small station or town.

family disturber: A pay car or pay train.

fan: The blower on a locomotive boiler. To get speed.

fantail: A switch engine with a sloping, flaring tender.

fan the door: To swing the fire door open and shut to create a draft.

fast freight: A through freight train with a speedy schedule.

fast mail: A fast passenger train.

fast roller: A fast engineer.

FAST TRAIN
    See [passenger] cannonball express, flyer,

greased lightning, highball, highliner, hotshot, lightning express, time-card train, [freight] ball of fire, dicer, hotshot freight, manifest, red ball, stinger.

feather-bed: To require an employer under a union rule or safety status to use and pay more employees than are needed.

feathers: Sleep. One's fingers.

feed stop: The stopping of a circus train to feed the animals. Before the day of dining cars, a town where a train stopped to feed the passengers.

feedwater heater: A heater that brought cold water from the tender almost to the boiling point before being pumped into the boiler.

ferrophiliac: An amateur of railroading and locomotives.

field: A classified railway yard.

fielder: A yard brakeman.

field man: A yard brakeman.

fight her: To feed fuel to a lagging locomotive.

figurehead: The timekeeper.

filling station: A water tank.

fill out: To add enough cars to a train to make up the full tonnage that the locomotive can pull over a given division of track.

fire: To throw a tramp off a train. To discharge an employee.

firebox: The engine fire chamber into which the fireman threw the coal to keep up steam.

fireboy: A fireman.

fire decks: A set of boards nailed to the ties of a bridge that are covered with tar and gravel to prevent fires caused by hot cinders.

fire door: The door in the firebox through which fuel is thrown on the fire.

fire feeder: A fireman.

fire flue: A tube in a steam boiler through which hot gases pass to heat the surrounding water.

fireman: A man whose duty it was to keep up steam by shoveling coal into the firebox, placing the coal evenly to prevent smoke. He sat on the left side of the cab, and it was his duty to watch that side of the track, ring the bell, keep the cab clean, wash the windows, and keep coal handy to the firebox. His job was also a hopeful apprenticeship for becoming an engineer. He also had to stoke the fire and maintain the water level in the boiler.

FIREMAN

> *See* ashcat, ash eater, ashpit engineer, bake head, banjo, bell-bottom brakeman, bellringer, blackie, clinker boy, coal heaver, coaly, crack the black diamonds, cut the buck, diamond heaver, diamond pusher, diamond thrower, dust raiser, fake head, fireboy, fireman, fireman's friend, goat feeder, grease ball, grease burner, handle the scoop, hang the fireman's hide on the coal gates, has lots of putty, Johnny-on-the-Spot, move dirt, push the spade, rathole artist, rawhide the fireman, scoop, smoke boy, soda jerker, stringer, stoker, stoke the hay burner, student smoke agent, student

tallow pot, tallow dip, tallow pot, throttle fever, throw away the diamonds, tool of ignorance, traveling man.

fire trains: A train with a fire pump mounted on an engine, with hose and tank cars of water for fighting fires; used mostly on logging trains.

first reader: The conductor's train book.

fish: To dislodge a tramp from the rods by dragging a piece of metal tied to a string under the car to make it rebound from the ties. A passenger.

fish belly: A short rail with a swelled undersurface that provides greater thickness between the ties above them, for uniform strength.

fish horn: An electric horn on an electric or gasoline railcar.

fish plate: A steel plate used to fasten the ends of rails together.

fishtail: A peculiarly shaped blade of a semaphore.

fish wagon: A gas-electric car or other motor car equipped with an air horn.

fist: A telegraph operator's handwriting. Though of necessity done swiftly, it was always legible. Anyone acquainted with it would immediately recognize it as the writing of a telegraph operator.

fixed man: A yard switchman placed at a fixed position from which he rode the cars to a designated place and back to their fixed place.

fixed signal: A derisive term for a student brakeman on top of a boxcar with his lantern out.

flag: To signal; when his train has made an unscheduled stop, the brakeman is sent back to protect the rear of the train. To work under an assumed name. A blacklisted boomer working under an assumed name.

flag a block: To go ahead of a train to signal oncoming trains.

flagman: A man hired to give signals at certain places.

FLAGMAN
　See drawbar flagging, flag, flagman, short flagging.

flange: A rim projecting from the inside edge of a wheel to guide it along the track.

flanger: An addition to a snow plow to remove the snow below the level of the rails that the snow plow itself does not reach.

flat: A flatcar. A hotcake.

flatcar: A freight car without sides, ends, or tops, used to haul many kinds of freight.

flatfoot: A railroad policeman.

flat wheel: A car wheel with a flat spot on the tread. A lame train employee.

flexible boiler: A boiler with two parts connected by a flexible boiler joint.

flexible boiler joint: A connection between the two parts of the flexible boiler, allowing the forward end to rotate when the locomotive rounds a curve.

flimsy: A train order, so called because it is written on tissue paper. An order written on transparent paper so that light passing through outlines the message.

flip: To board a moving train.

flipper: A stowaway.

flip tissues: To look over train orders. Also *flop tissues.*

floater: A *boomer (q.v.).* A migratory railroad worker.

floating buffer: A connection between the engine and the tender to allow space for the engine to attain sharp curves.

floating gang: A section gang living in boxcars made into living quarters to move them quickly to any spot of emergency.

flop: A bed.

flophouse: A caboose. A cheap hotel.

flue: A fire tube.

fly-ball governor: An automatic contrivance to slow by centrifugal force the speed of an engine running faster than the desired speed.

flyer: A fast train; usually applied to passenger trains.

fly in: To switch a car by a *flying switch (q.v.).*

flying squadron: The first section of a circus train.

flying switch: A form of switching by which the engine pulls rapidly away from the car or cars which it has started in motion, allowing them to be switched to a different track from that taken by the engine. A switchman is there to throw the switch as soon as the engine has passed and just before the cars reach it. After the original start the engine greatly increases its speed to pass the switch and allow the switchman time to throw the switch before the cars arrive.

fly light: To miss a meal before going to work. To run an engine without cars or with a very few cars.

flywheel: A large wheel on the crankshaft of an engine to convert oscillating action to a smooth rotative force.

foam: To take water with live steam in the cylinders.

fog: To travel under full steam.

fog up: To produce steam.

follower plate: A piece of iron about fourteen inches square and one inch thick with a hole in the center.

FOOD

    See beanery, beanery queen, beans, blind gasket, collar-and-elbow joint, crown sheet, flat, flatcar, grazing ticket, hasher, hash house, jailhouse spuds, jam nute, lizard scorcher, meal book, nosebag, nule, pearl diver, peck, pie book, pie card, puncher, put on the nosebag, red onion, rolling stock, switch list, take your minutes, torpedo, whitewash.

footboard: The step on the front or rear end of a switch engine. Missing these steps on an icy or stormy night is extremely dangerous.

footboard yardmaster: The foreman of the yard switchmen.

foreign car: A car from a railroad other than the one using it.

foreign run: A run that ends away from a terminal.

Forney-type engine: A locomotive carrying fuel and water in the receptacles and tanks part of the engine rather than in the tender.

forty-eight bucket: A large lunch pail used in the old days for extralarge lunches to last for long trips.

forty-five signal: A signal with a mechanical arm that provides information on the proximity of trains immediately ahead.

foul the train: Said of a car on a siding that extends onto the main line.

fountain: That part of a locomotive where the steam issues from the boiler and flows into the pipes.

fourth man: An additional brakeman.

fox: One who rides inside passenger cars.

frazzled: Drunk.

freeze: To cool an overheated journal.

freeze a blazer: To cool an overheated journal.

freezer: A refrigerator car.

freeze the hub: To cool an overheated journal.

freight car: A car with top, sides, ends, and a sliding door on each side, used for hauling freight.

FREIGHT CAR

> *See* arms horse car, ballast car, blackjack, black one, blacksnake, boxcar, carhouse car, chisel, coaler, coal eight, cow crate, cradle, donegan, double-decked stock, elephant car, flatcar, freezer car, freight car, glory, gon, gooseneck, gunboat, hopper, house car, icer, idler, jimmy, Johnny O'Brien, lee of a reefer, load, oil car, oiler, old pelican, palace sleeper, parlor car, riff, side-door Pullman, slip, sowbelly, steel boy, stock, stock car, stoker, straight spout, vent wagon, whale belly, Zulu car.

freighter: A freight train.

freight shacks: A freight-train crew.

fresh fish: A green hand.

fresh-water town: A small station or town.

friction wheel: A wheel-and-action assembly that rotates as one.

fried: Drunk.

frog: An X-shaped metal plate of a crossover. An implement for derailing car wheels. A device permitting the wheels on one rail to cross an intersecting rail.

front shack: A front brakeman.

fuel bunker: The coal section of the tender. A section in a locomotive for holding fuel.

fumble the hoop: To miss the hoop upon which train orders are attached when passing a station.

fusee: A tube used for signaling, containing potassium dichromate and sulfur and sand and with a sharp spike attached to the end. Thrown so that the spike sticks into a tie, it burns in the desired color of red, yellow, or green about fifteen minutes to signal a closely following train to slow down and proceed with caution. It must be able to burn in rain or snow.

gab hook: A part of the valve-gear mechanism on an early locomotive.

gaffer: A section boss.

gage cock: One of three valves, each one located on a level about three inches lower than the other. By opening the top valve, steam or water would come out of the opening, depending upon the level of water in the boiler. If the lower valve showed steam instead of water, the engineer would know he was dangerously low on water. This system was a double check on the water-glass indicator.

galloper: A locomotive. An iron horse.

galloping goose: A shaky section car. A caboose.

galloping rod: A diesel-electric connecting rod.

galvanizer: A car inspector.

gandy dancer: A track laborer, so called from the Gandy Manufacturing Company of Chicago, which made many of the tools used by the section gangs.

gandy gang: A section gang.

gang buster: An agitator in a section gang.

gang pusher: A section boss.

gangway: The space between the rear cab post of a locomotive and the tender.

garden: A railroad yard.

gas house: A yard office.

gasket: A doughnut.

gate: A switch. A derailer.

gay cat: A hobo held in contempt by his fellow tramps because of his willingness to work if offered a job.

geared engine: A locomotive in which the power from the cylinders is transmitted to the wheels through gears.

gear train: A group of gears having intermeshed teeth, used to increase or decrease rotative speed.

general: A yardmaster.

George: A train porter.

getaway: A locomotive.

get a lung: To uncouple or pull a drawbar.

get her hide tight: To get up steam.

get the engine hot: To build up a fire in the engine to produce a working steam.

get the rocking chair: To retire on a pension.

get your head cut in: To "get wise," said by a *boomer (q.v.).*

gig top: An early-day shelter on top of a fuel car for the brakeman, the upper section being canvas stretched over bows.

giraffe: A mining car higher at one end than at the

other, used on inclines.

girl: A locomotive. Like a ship, a locomotive is referred to as "she" or "her."

give her a drink: To take on water.

give her the air: To apply air brakes.

give her the grit: To use sand on the track to prevent slipping or to gain traction.

give her the one: To make an emergency stop.

give her the works: To make an emergency stop.

give running repairs: To overhaul a damaged car on the repair track.

give the old girl a dose of salts: See *dust her out*.

glass car: A passenger car.

glass of water: Said when the water gauge indicates the highest water level. At this level the engine works without carrying water with live steam to the cylinders.

glim: A switchman's or trainman's lantern.

glimmer: A locomotive headlight.

glory: A string of empty cars. Death, especially by accident.

glory hunter: A reckless, fast-running engineer.

glory road: A sentimental term for a railroad.

glory wagon: A caboose.

G.M.: Short for *general manager*.

goat: A yard engine, so called because it butts cars around the yard.

goat feeder: A yard fireman.

goat herder: A yard engineer.

go-cart: A caboose.

go dead: To reach the sixteen-hour work limit prescribed by law.

go devil: A handcar.

god of iron: A huge, powerful engine.

go fishing: To lay off from work.

go high: To climb to the top of a freight car to signal or set brakes.

gold buttons: A conductor.

go light: To run an engine only, without cars.

go in the hole: To go onto a side track.

gon: Short for *gondola*, a steel-sided, flat-bottom coal car.

GO OFF DUTY
> *See* go fishing, join the birds, pin for home, tie up, unload, pull the pin, on the spot, unload.

goo-goo eyes: A locomotive with two fire doors.

go on the carpet: To go before superiors for some infraction of the rules.

go on the farm: To go onto a side track.

goose: A switchman. To make an emergency stop.

goose her: To reverse a locomotive when under headway.

gooseneck: An oil can with a special type of pipe connection.

gooseneck coupling link: A bent link used in the days of the link-and-pin coupling, in which one coupling was somewhat higher than the other.

go through: To go to a destination without a stop-over.

go to the hammer track: To go on the *rip track (q.v.)* for repairs.

go-to-hell signal: A signal given with a violent motion of hand or lantern.

governor: An automatic device to set a limit on speed.

grabber: A conductor, so called because he grabs tickets.

grab a few wagons: To pick up a few cars.

grab a handful of boxcar: To board a moving freight train.

grab iron: A steel bar attached to a car or engine for a handhold.

grab one's car numbers: To enter car numbers in a train book.

grade crossing: A logging car with a bulkhead at one end to prevent the loss of logs on incline railroads.

gramophone: A telephone.

grandpa: A general manager.

grasshopper-type engine: An early-day engine, so called from the motion of its walking beams and its long rods, which resembled a grasshopper's hind legs.

grass wagon: A tourist car.

grate: A set of parallel bars at the bottom of the firebox to hold the fuel.

gravedigger: A section man.

graveyard: A siding used for outmoded and unused engines and cars. A scrap pile.

graveyard shift: A work period from 12:01 A.M. to 8:00 A.M. Any midnight shift, so called because these are the quietest hours. Also called *graveyard watch, gray eye.*

graveyard watch: See *graveyard shift.*

gray eye: See *graveyard shift.*

gravy run: A short, easy haul. Also called *gravy train.*

gravy train: See *gravy run.*

grazing ticket: A railroader's meal book.

grease ball: A mechanic. A fireman.

grease burner: A fireman on a crude oil locomotive.

greased lightning: A fast train.

grease monkey: A car oiler.

grease pot: Butter.

grease the pig: To oil the engine.

grease the track: To be run over by a train.

greasy spoon: A railroad eating house.

greenback: A frog for derailing cars or engines. A similar device forming a connection with another track.

green-ball freight: A freight train whose cargo is fruit or vegetables.

green carrier: The first section of a two-part train, so called because it carries a green flag or green light.

green eye: A clear signal.

green light: A green traffic signal giving permission to proceed.

greetings from the DS: Train orders from the dispatcher.

grid: A gridiron track.

griever: A spokesman for a grievance committee. A union representative at an official investigation.

grind: A Shay-geared engine.

grips: A passenger porter.

grit: Sand used to increase traction on slippery rails.

groundhog: A brakeman. A yardmaster. A switch engine.

grout: To pump a mixture of sand and cement into the roadbed to strengthen soft spots.

grunt: A locomotive engineer. A lineman's helper. To work as a lineman's helper.

gumshoe: A railroad detective, so called because in the early days he wore gum-soled shoes.

gun: The injector on a locomotive that forces water from tank to boiler. A torpedo placed on the track for signaling and a part of the trainman's equipment. To control the air brakes from the rear of the train.

gunboat: A large steel car.

gunnel stiff: One who *rides 'em high (q.v.).*

gut: An air hose.

guts: A drawbar.

G.Y.M.: Short for *general yardmaster.*

gypsy: A locomotive with steam-powered winches, used to fetch logs.

hack: A caboose.

half: A trainman's period of two weeks.

ham: A poor telegraph operator. A student operator.

hand bomber: A hand-fired engine without an automatic stoker. Also called *hand grenade*.

hand car: A flat truck with four wheels propelled by a two-handled pump. It was used in the early days to carry section crews to work and back to the section house. It was light enough to be lifted off the track to avoid a collision with a passing train. Later gasoline cars were used, especially for the track inspector.

hand grenade: See *hand bomber*.

handle the scoop: To work as a fireman.

hand-on: A train order caught with a hoop by a passing trainman.

hand shoe: A glove.

hang the fireman's hide on the coal gate: To overwork the fireman.

hand up the clock: To hock a railroad watch, a term

used by a *boomer (q.v.).*

hard-coaler: A railroad that hauls a lot of anthracite coal.

harness: A passenger trainman's uniform.

hasher: A waitress in a railroad eating house.

has his head cut in: Sensible; said of a man who is as much under control as a train with its air brakes cut in.

hash house: A railroad restaurant or lunchroom.

has lots of putty: Said of a fireman when the steam gauge shows full working power.

hat: A railroader who is ineffectual. It is said that he uses his head for a hatrack.

have a feather out: To release wisps of steam from the safety valve.

have it up against the brass: To get speed from an engine.

hay: To sleep on the job.

hay burner: A hand oil lantern. A worn-out locomotive.

hay shaker: A cowboy who accompanies a cattle shipment.

haystack boiler: A boiler featuring a large dome above the furnace resembling a haystack.

hay wagon: A caboose.

head brakeman: A brakeman whose duty is to ride at the head of the train, open and close switches, help oil valves and take on water, act as flagman, and run ahead to protect the front of the train.

head end: The front of a train or locomotive.

head-end: To pull a train.

head-ender: A head-on collision, a wreck all railroaders dread.

header: A two-compartment reservoir occupying part of the smokebox.

head in: To take a side track when meeting an opposing train.

head-in revenue: Money the railroad receives for hauling mail, express, newspapers, baggage, and other such articles in the baggage and mail cars; also called *head-on traffic.*

head man: A front brakeman on a freight train who rides in the engine cab.

head-on: A head-on collision. To move with the engine forward.

head-on traffic: See *head-in revenue.*

head pin: A front brakeman on a freight train who rides the engine.

head shack: A front brakeman.

hearse: A caboose.

heel: Cars on the end of a track with the brakes applied.

heist: To throw a tramp off the train.

held up by the blue flag: Said of a train detained for inspection or repairs.

Hell Either Way You Take It: The Houston, East & West Texas Railway.

hell on wheels: An expression originating during the

building of the Union Pacific Railway in 1867. As the rails were laid westward, the honkytonks, gambling hells (buildings and all), and harlots were loaded on flatcars and moved to the new terminal. All the town's hell was then on wheels.

helper: An auxiliary engine in a double-header to help trains on steep grades or those with extra-heavy loads.

helper engine: A second engine to help the single engine pull its load over a section of mountain or other track.

herald: A device, monogram, or other symbol of a railroad company, usually used as an identifying marker on freight cars.

herder: A man who couples or uncouples engines and takes them off upon arrival or departure of trains. A section boss.

herd the calliope: To follow the engine; said of the yard switchman.

herd the pig: See *herd the calliope.*

herd the stove: See *herd the calliope.*

hickey: A metal bundle used by brakemen in setting hand brakes (though most of them used a hardwood stick).

highball: A signal given by the conductor or brakeman by waving a hand or lantern in a high, wide semicircle, meaning "leave town" or "full speed ahead."

highball artist: A locomotive engineer known for running fast.

highball camp: A road camp in which men are worked

at full speed. Also called *highball outfit*.

highball outfit: See *highball camp*.

highball the switch: To fail to slow down for the brakeman to close the switch, leaving it to the yard switchman.

high brass: The high officials of the railroad.

high daddy: A flying switch.

High Grass: A name given the Central New England Railroad.

high hat: A big steel gondola car.

high iron: The main line. High-speed track laid with heavier rails than those used by branches and spurs.

high-iron dog: A passenger train.

highline: The main track.

highliner: A mainline passenger train.

high-pressure engine: An engine with pistons driven directly by the expansive force of steam.

high stepper: A fast engine with tall drivers.

high-tail: To depart at rapid speed.

high-wheeler: A locomotive with very large driving wheels for greater speed. A fast passenger train. A *highball artist (q.v.)*.

hiker: A lineman who "hikes sticks" instead of climbing poles.

hind hook: A rear brakeman; also called *hind shack*.

hind shack: See *hind hook*.

hitch: To couple cars.

hitch up the iron mule: To couple a donkey engine

to a car.

hit 'er: To work an engine harder.

hit the ball: To get speed.

hit the brush: To jump off a runaway train.

hit the cinders: To walk the track. To jump off a moving train.

hit the cinder trail: To walk the track.

hit the dirt: To be thrown off a train. To jump or fall from a moving train.

hit the gravel: See *hit the dirt.*

hit the grit: See *hit the dirt.*

hit the high spots: To go at great speed.

hit the pike: To hike down the railroad track toward town.

hit the steel: See *hit the pike.*

hobo: A tramp. A steam coal pusher used to push the coal up to the fireman.

HOBO

See bindle stiff, blanket stiff, blind baggage, blind men, bo, bomb, bo money, bo park, box-car artist, bo yard, box tourist, bum-sick train, catter, cinder, cinder grifter, cinder sifter, cinder trail, crum bundle, dangler, dewdrop, ditch, fire, fish, gay cat, gunnel stiff, heist, hit the dirt, hit the gravel, hit the grit, hobo, hobo land, hobo limited, hobo short line, hunger lane, jumper tramp, jungle buzzard, open-air navigator, red light, ride the blinds, ride the bumpers, ride the rods, ringtail, rodman, rustle the bums, side-door Pullman, slough, snake a stiff, tie pass, tough road, track stiff, train chaser, tramp ticket, trapeze artist, trespasser.

hobo land: A train with a crew friendly to tramps. Also called *hobo limited.*

hobo limited: See *hobo land.*

hobo short line: Death or suicide by being run over by a train.

hog: A locomotive with an extralarge boiler. Any engine.

hogback: The top of a hill.

hog eye: An engineer; also called *hogger, hoghead, hogineer, hog jerker, hog jockey.*

hogger: See *hog eye.*

hog jerker: See *hog eye.*

hog jockey: See *hog eye.*

hog law: A crew sent out to relieve another that has been overtaken by the ICC sixteen-hour regulation.

hog law's got 'em: Said of a crew that has been on duty the full sixteen-hour work period.

hogmaster: An engineer; also called *hog mauler.*

hog mauler: See *hogmaster.*

hold 'em up: To brake.

hold her against the brass: To run an electric car at full speed.

hole: A switch where one train pulls in to meet another. A passing track. In logging, the area between the loads where the brakeman stood to apply the brakes.

hole in the boiler: An ulcer; said of one who has a stomach ailment.

home guard: An employee who stays with one railroad, as contrasted with a *boomer (q.v.)*.

homestead: To jump off a runaway train.

homesteader: A *boomer (q.v.)* who gets married and settles down.

home talent: A locally recruited mechanic, particularly one used on moving gangs.

honey train: A fruit train.

hook: A wrecking crane. An eating fork.

hook 'er up and pull 'er tail: To set the reverse lever up on the quadrant and pull the throttle out for high speed. When speed is attained, to raise the reverse lever toward the center of its quadrant to permit quick admission and exhaust the steam.

hook up: To set the reverse lever toward the top center on the quadrant for speed. To couple cars.

hoop: A metal device for catching orders on the run.

hop: A passenger-train porter.

hopper: A steel-sided car with a bottom that opens to allow unloading of such freight as gravel and coal by gravity.

hoptoad: A derailer on a railroad switch to prevent cars from running out on the main track.

horse 'er over: To reverse the engine.

hose coupler: A brakeman who handles trains alone with a road engine around a large passenger terminal.

hostler: An employee who services engines at division points and terminals. A tender of the roundhouse. One whose job it is to move engines in and out of the roundhouse.

hot: A live engine. Having plenty of steam pressure in a locomotive.

hotbox: An overheated journal. Also called *hot jewel*. In the early days of railroading overheated journals often delayed trains; modern cars are equipped with ball bearings. A passionate girl.

hotbox detector: A trainman.

hotbox dick: A car inspector. A repairman.

hotcake: See *blind gasket, flatcar, flat*.

hot-footer: An engineer or conductor in switching service who is always in a hurry.

hot jewel: See *hotbox*.

hot rail: A warning that a train is coming and to clear the track.

hot-rodder: A fast engineer.

hotshot: A fast train. A freight carrying perishables.

hotshot freight: A fast freight train.

hot-water bottle: A feedwater heater.

hot worker: A boilermaker who repairs leaks in the firebox or flue sheet while there is pressure in the boiler.

house car: A boxcar.

house track: A track alongside a station for loading and unloading passengers or freight; also called *station track*.

How many ems have you got?: An expression meaning, "How many thousand pounds of tonnage is your engine pulling?"

Hudson-type engine: A 4-6-4 wheel-arrangement locomotive.

hump: A man-made knoll at the end of a freight yard over which cars are pushed to enable them to roll on their own momentum to other tracks. The top of a hill division to the top of a prominent grade.

humpback: A piece of metal spiked to the ties, used to guide the wheels of a derailed car back onto the track.

hump-backed hog: A consolidation-type locomotive.

humpback job: A local freight run, so called because the conductor spends most of his time in the caboose "humping" over his reports.

humpback run: A local freight run.

hump brakie: The switchman or brakeman who handles cars on the yard gravity tracks.

hump yard: A railroad yard on an incline, making it easier for cars to be switched by their own gravity after being cut loose from the engine.

hunger lane: A tramp expression for a railroad in a poor, unfriendly district.

independent air: Air brakes on locomotives separate from the trainline brakes.

independent system: A braking system using momentum as a slowing force.

indicator: An illuminated sign on both the engine and the caboose that shows the train's number. A watch.

Indian Valley Line: Death, or the railroader's heaven, where there was always a good job open with excellent working conditions.

injector: An appliance by which water could be added to the boiler. The engineer's injector provided water for the boiler when the demand was more than the fireman's injector could handle or when the fireman's injector failed.

inside: An inside passenger.

intercepting valve: A valve that delivers high-pressure steam to all cylinders at starting. As the need for tractive effort decreases, its passages are realigned for compound operation.

in the clear: A train that has cleared a switch far

enough that another train can pass without hitting it.

in the color: Said of a train standing in a signal block waiting for a clear board.

in the corner: Said of the Johnson bar of the engine, which, when shoved ahead to its last notch, was in the right-hand corner of the cab, making the engine pull harder.

in the ditch: Said of a wrecked train.

in the hole: On a siding. Said of a lower berth on a Pullman.

iron: A railroad track. *Single iron* means single track.

iron bender: A brakeman or switchman.

iron fireman: An automatic stoker.

iron hog: A locomotive.

iron horse: A locomotive.

iron man: An automatic stoker. A track layer.

iron operator: An amplifying telephone transmitter to record trains passing unattended stations.

iron skull: A boilermaker.

jack: A locomotive. A lifting jack.

jackpot: Mail and parcels piled in the aisles of a baggage car.

jailhouse spuds: Waffled potatoes.

jam buster: An assistant yardmaster.

jam nut: A doughnut.

janney: A switch shanty.

Janney coupler: A coupler that took the place of the old link-and-pin coupler, so called for its inventor. It was a godsend to trainmen, saving their hands and fingers.

jawbone shack: A switch shack, evidently so called because so much talking went on there.

jay rod: A clinker hook used by the fireman.

jerk-by: A flying switch.

jerk a drink: To take water from a track pan without stopping the train, a method used by some of the eastern railroads.

jerk soup: See *jerk a drink*.

jerkwater: A small town. A local train.

jerry: A section worker.

jerry gang: A section crew.

jewel: Journal brass.

jigger: A full tonnage of dead freight. A slow freight train.

jiggerooski: A yardmaster.

jill poke: A stout pole used to shove cars out of a siding when the engine is working on the main line and cannot lead to pick up the cars. Also called *jill pole.*

jill pole: See *jill poke.*

Jim Crow: An instrument for straightening rails.

jimmy: A four-wheel coal or ore car.

jingle the brass: To ring the locomotive bell.

jitney: An electric truck for carrying baggage at a terminal.

job: A locomotive.

jockey: A yard switchman who rides cars.

Johnny O'Brien: A boxcar.

Johnny-on-the-spot: A fireman who keeps the steam pressure to the red spot.

Johnson bar: The reverse lever of a locomotive.

joint: A length of rail, usually 33 to 39 feet.

jointed boiler: A *flexible boiler (q.v.).*

join the birds: To jump from a moving engine or car, usually when a wreck is imminent. To go off duty.

journal: The part of a rotating shaft or axle that turns in a shaft. The external bearing area on the end of the axle.

journal box: An iron box that protects and supports the journal bearing.

journal hook: A tool used to open journal-box covers.

juggler: A member of a way-freight crew who load and unload freight at station stops. A brakeman.

juggle the circle: To miss a train-order hoop.

juice: Water. The electricity that runs an electric train.

jumper: A stowaway.

jumper tramp: A tramp who steals rides on trains.

jumping-off place: A small station or town.

jungle buzzard: A hobo.

junk file: An old, worn-out locomotive that is still in service.

kangaroo court: An investigation of a worker by officials, so called because it is held anywhere along the road.

Katy: The Missouri, Kansas & Texas Railroad.

Keeley: A small water tank hung on the side of a car and attached to a hose, to be used in case of *hotbox (q.v.).*

keep the engine hot: To keep the steam where it belongs.

keester: A suitcase or trunk.

keester keeper: A baggage man.

kettle: A small locomotive.

kettle mender: A boilermaker. A roundhouse machinist.

key: A telegraph instrument.

kick: To uncouple cars while they are in motion, allowing them to roll to a selected spot.

kicker: A triple valve that throws air brakes into service, especially a defective one.

kick signal: A signal given by holding out the arm

and moving the hand rapidly up and down.

kick up the pops: To set the pressure valves on the air system.

Killingsworth-type engine: A locomotive with four drivers, originally used in England to haul coal from the Killingsworth mines.

king: A yardmaster. A freight conductor.

king pin: A conductor.

king snipe: The foreman of a track or section gang.

kink: A section of poorly ballasted track warped by the sun.

kipps: A caboose.

kitchen: A caboose, so called because the crews' meals are prepared in it en route. A locomotive cab, so called because of its heat.

kitchen car: The cook car of a railroad camp.

kitchen stove: The firebox of the boiler.

knock a foul: To strike a car that is not clear on a siding.

knock down: To steal fares from the company.

knock it: To demote a worker. To take the turn of another railroader.

knockout: To obtain another's job by exercising one's seniority.

knock the fire: To shake the grate and dump the ash pan into the ash pit.

knowledge box: The yardman's office. The president of the road.

knuckle buster: A mechanic.

knuckle coupler: An automatic coupler that took the place of the link-and-pin coupler, eliminating many of the dangers in coupling cars.

ladder: The main yard track from which other tracks lead off.

lagging: An insulated covering on the outside of the boiler and the cylinders to hold in the heat.

lake shore: The sand in the sand dome that is used for traction.

lamb's tongue: A fifty-cent tip.

lampblack: Coal.

lap: A section of track owned by more than one company.

laplander: A passenger jostled into another's lap when a car is crowded and the ride is rough.

lap order: A mistake in train orders.

lap the brake valve: To position the brake control to hold the existing application constant.

last call: Death.

last terminal: Death.

latch: The locomotive throttle.

lateral-play axle: An axle that allows flanged wheels

to move from one side to another, adjusting themselves to curves.

lay-by: A side track.

layed out: Delayed or sidetracked.

layover: Time spent waiting for connection with another train.

lay-up: A stopover.

LCL: Short for *less than carload lots* of freight.

lead: The main track in a yard from which other tracks lead off. The amount a valve moves at the start of a piston stroke.

lead spring: A multiple spring made of several layers of spring metal bracketed together.

leave the gate: To leave the closing of a switch to a yard switchman instead of slowing the train for a brakeman to perform the task.

lee of a reefer: The ice compartment in a refrigerator car.

leg: A section of a rail journey.

letters: Letters given to an employee who has quit or been laid off showing future employers that he has had experience.

lever jerker: An interlocker man.

library: The cupola of a caboose.

librarian: A trainman occupying the cupola.

lid: An inefficient telegraph operator.

lift: To raise a track and ballast it.

lift the rivet: To pull a drawbar, or uncouple cars.

lift transportation: To collect fares.

light engine: An engine without cars going outside the yard.

lightning express: A fast train, usually a passenger train.

lightning slinger: A fast telegraph operator.

limited: A train pulling a limited number of cars and making a limited number of stops. A train offering the best and fastest service.

lincoln pin: A *link-and-pin coupler (q.v.).*

liner: A luxury passenger train.

line 'er up: To fire up the engine.

link: A piece of crescent-shaped metal in the valve gear having a central slot that accommodates a sliding block fastened to the valve rod.

link-and-pin coupler: An old-time coupler formed of an iron link and two pins.

Little Nemo: An extra engine. Whisky.

live number: Any living freight, man or animal.

lizard scorcher: A dining-car chef. A cook for a section gang.

load: A loaded freight car.

local load: A truckload of mail and parcels from storage to a car of a local train. Mail to be delivered along the train's route.

loco: Short for *locomotive.*

locomotive: An engine that runs on rails and pulls the cars that make up the train.

LOCOMOTIVE

See Armstrong, battleship, battle wagon, blood, bobtail, boiler, bowling alley, bull, bullgine, bus, cab, calliope, camel, camelback, coaler, coffeepot, couldn't pull a settin' hen off the nest, dead engine, deck, deck kitchen, dinky, drill, duster, eight-wheeler, engine, fantail, fountain, galloper, getaway, girl, goat, god of iron, goo-goo eyes, grasshopper, grind, groundhog, hand bomber, helper, high-wheeler, hog, hump-backed hog, iron hog, iron horse, job, junk pile, kettle, Little Nemo, loco, locomotive, locomotive cord, lokey, mallet, mill, mill kettle, Mother Hubbard, mudhen, muzzle-loader, oiler, old girl, old pelican, paddle wheel, peanut roaster, pig, pig iron, pony, pony engine, pot, power, puller, rammer, rat crusher, roof garden, rust pile, sacred cow, sacred ox, scrap pile, shunting boiler, side-wheeler, sidewinder, smoker, smokolotive, snap, snapper, snuff dipper, soak, stack of rust, steam horse, steam wagon, stem-winder, switch engine, tank, tea-kettle, teapot, tender, ting-a-ling, tramp, trimmer, work steam.

locomotive cord: In the early days of wood-burning engines, wood for fuel cut two feet long and piled into cord stacks along the tracks.

logging car: A railroad car used for hauling logs.

lokey: Short for *locomotive*.

lokey man: An engineer.

lone wolf: A nonbrotherhood man; also called *wolf*.

long whiskers: A man with long seniority.

lost his nerve: Said of one who planned to swing onto a moving train but decided it was traveling too fast.

lounge car: A passenger car with seats for lounging and facilities for serving refreshments.

louse cage: A caboose.

lower berth: The bottom berth of a Pullman car. The underbracings of a railway car.

lower deck: The front platform of a baggage car where there is no door.

lowering rig: An engine used to raise or lower log cars on an incline.

lug: Short for *luggage*.

lumper: A freight-shed laborer.

lump oil: Coal.

lunar white: The shade of white used on all switches except the main line.

lunch hooks: The railroader's term for his hands.

lung: A drawbar or air hose.

lung doctor: An engineer who pulls out drawbars.

lung jerker: A careless or heavy-handed engineer; also called *lung specialist*.

lying dead: Said of a train that has come to a stop.

madhouse: The engine foreman. The roundhouse, where there is an unusual amount of activity. A caboose.

MAIL

> *See* mail clerk, nixie, paper jerker, separation, set up, sleeper, slug, terminal load, two-wheeler, Uncle Sam.

mail clerk: A man who handles mail for the government on trains and at the station mail office.

main iron: A main track.

main line: A main track.

main liner: An engineer working on the *main line (q.v.).*

main pin: An official. A railroad superintendent.

main reservoir: An iron tank for the storage of compressed air used in the air-brake system.

main rod: The big steel rod used to transmit the motion of the piston and piston rod to the large driver wheels of the locomotive.

main steel: A main track.

main stem: A main track.

main street: A main track.

main track: The principal track of the railroad.

MAIN TRACK
> *See* high iron, high line, main iron, main line, main steel, main stem, main street, main track.

make a hitch: To couple cars.

make a joint: To couple cars.

make money fast: Said of the crew on a fast passenger train.

make out a single track: To make out an accident report.

make up: To assemble cars into a train.

Mallet: A compound articulated engine, named for its Swiss inventor, Anatole Mallet.

maniac: A mechanic.

manifest: A fast freight train hauling perishables or livestock.

marker: A signal. When a train is on the main line, certain signals must be shown. A red light is shown in the front and rear of the train, and a green light is shown on the side. After the train goes into the clear, the lights are green in the front and rear and red on the side.

master: A conductor.

master car repairer: A man who reports directly to the master mechanic for his duties.

master maniac: A master mechanic in charge of the mechanics department of an operating division.

master mechanic: A man responsible for the maintenance of the mechanics equipment, shop, and shop machinery and for the repair and rebuilding of engines. He had to provide the motor power that kept the trains rolling.

master mechanic's blood: A master mechanic's oil.

master mind: An official. A trainmaster. A conductor.

mastodon-type engine: A 4-8-0 locomotive that used steam cylinders to actuate the reversing levers and the valve gear.

match dials: To compare watches, as when the engineer and the conductor compare the time.

match watches: See *match dials.*

mail: To work an engine with a full stroke and throttle.

MCB: The automatic coupler that took the place of the old link-and-pin coupler and became universal in 1888. It was based on the principle of the hooked fingers of the human hand.

meal-a-mat: A food vending machine on some trains instead of a dining car. Similar to a coin cigarette machine, it offered various foods at designated prices.

meal book: A railroader's book of meal tickets.

MEAL TICKET
> *See* grazing ticket, meal book, pie card.

meat run: A fast run of perishable freight; also called *hotshot.*

MECHANIC
> *See* chambermaid, grease ball, home talent, knuckle buster, master maniac, master me-

chanic, master mechanic's blood, nut cracker, nut splitter, thumb buster, wrench artist.

meet order: A train order naming a specific location at which two or more trains will meet, one on a siding, the other on the main line.

merchandise peddler: A way freight train; see *way car.*

merchandiser: A train hauling freight other than bulk commodities.

merry-go-round: The roundhouse turntable.

middle man: The second brakeman on a freight train; also called *middle swing.*

middle swing: See *middle man.*

mighty mogul: An extralarge 2-6-0 engine.

Mikado-type engine: A 2-8-2 locomotive produced by the Baldwin Locomotive Works for Japan's Nippon Railway in 1897 and used for a time in the United States.

Mike: Short for *Mikado-type engine (q.v.).*

mileage hog: An engineer or conductor paid by mileage who used his seniority to secure the best runs.

mile post: A post indicating the distance in miles from a given point.

milk truck: A large hand truck with iron wheels used around the terminal to haul milk cans.

mill: A steam locomotive. A typewriter.

mill kettle: A locomotive.

minute miser: A train dispatcher.

Misery and Short Life: The Minneapolis and St. Louis Railroad.

mixed load: A truckload of mail sacks and parcels sent from the *storage car (q.v.)* to the yard. An outside platform for further mail separation before forwarding.

mixed train: A train made up of both passenger and freight cars.

mix me a tie pass: To hike down the railroad track to town.

Modoc: An employee train.

mogul: See *mighty mogul.*

money train: A fruit train.

money wagon: A *pay car (q.v.).*

monitor: The lookout box on a caboose.

monkey got 'em: Caught on the road after sixteen hours. See *hog law.*

monkey cage: A caboose; also called *monkey house, monkey hut, monkey wagon.*

monkey money: A passenger's free pass.

monkey motion: The Walschaert or Baker valve gear on a locomotive, so called because the eccentric rods shuttle back and forth with a curious hop at the end of each stroke.

monkey suit: A passenger trainman's uniform.

monkey tail: A back-up hose.

monkey wagon: A caboose.

moonlight mechanic: A roundhouse night foreman.

MOP: The Missouri Pacific Railroad.

mopping off: An expression describing escaping steam.

Mother Hubbard: An engine with a cab built over the middle of the boiler; also called *camelback*.

motion: The visible driving gear of a locomotive: the cross heads, side and main rods, link blocks, and so on.

motor: An electric locomotive.

mountain pay: Overtime.

mountain-type engine: A large 4-8-2 locomotive first used in 1911 for fast freights and passenger service.

move dirt: To shovel coal into the firebox.

moving car: A car built for moving heavy machinery, buildings on skids, and so on.

moving spirit: A train dispatcher.

mtys: Short for *empties*, empty cars.

mucker: An excavator in construction work.

muck-stick artist: A member of the section crew.

mudcap: To dynamite with mud. When, after a mud and rock slide, there are rocks too large to be moved by hand, dynamite is placed on top and covered with wet mud, then detonated.

mud chicken: A surveyor.

mud-digger engine: An early-day 0-8-0 locomotive, so called because its rough action caused mud to well up between the ties in wet weather.

mudhen: A saturated locomotive, one that is not superheated.

mudhole: A small station or town.

mud hop: A yard clerk. A car checker who lists the cars in arriving and departing trains.

mudscow: See *mike.*

mudshop: A nonlifting injection. A surveyor's office.

mudsucker: A nonlifting injector.

mule: A brakeman.

Mulligan car: A logging and crew car used in the early days for carrying hot meals to the woods crew at noon.

musicmaster: A paymaster.

Mutt-and-Jeff pump: A Denver and Rio Grande locomotive with a big air pump on the right and a small one on the left.

mutton head: A dispatcher.

muzzle-loader: A hand-fired locomotive.

muzzle-loading car: In logging, a rail-camp car with a door at the end, used as an office or commissary.

nail rattler: To board a moving train.

nail her on the fly: To board a moving train.

narrow gauge: A railroad with rails less than 4 feet, 8½ inches wide, narrower than the standard gauge used in early railroading.

new rail: A novice in railroading.

news butch: A salesman on an early-day passenger train who sold candy, fruit, newspapers, magazines, and other items. In selling his wares, he would entice a child accompanied by a parent with a glass pistol filled with colored candy pellets. As he passed down the aisle, the smell of bananas and oranges was very tempting. He tried to sell male passengers pornographic books on the sly. He would go through with salted peanuts and then, after they created a thirst, he would follow with cold bottled drinks. He did not fail to gather up all the used newspapers for resale or credit at the end of his route.

NEWS BUTCH
   See butch, candy butch, news butch.

niggerhead: A turret at the top of the locomotive boiler, over the crown sheet, from which saturated steam was taken for the operation of the pumps, stokers, injectors, and headlight turbine. A type of automatic signal.

nigger heaven: The top of a boxcar.

nigger local: A local freight train that involves much work for the crew.

nigger tip: A tip between fifteen and fifty cents.

nighthawk: A railroad detective disguised as a tramp.

night owl: A late passenger train.

nineteen order: A train order that did not require signing; the operator could hang it on a hook without having the train stopped.

ninety-nine: Failure to protect one's train or to flag it.

nipper: A brakeman. A track layer who holds up the ties being spiked to rails.

nip the pin: To uncouple or pull the drawbar. To stop, quit, or leave.

nixie: A railroad mail clerk term for an unsortable, misaddressed letter.

no-air: A car without a bill of lading. A nonunion worker.

no-bill: A car without a bill of lading.

non-air car: A freight car without air brakes.

no-nothing stop: A stop at a junction.

nosebag: A lunch bucket or bag carried to work.

nose on: To couple on with the head end of the engine.

Now you're railroading: An expression of commendation.

nule: The fourth black waiter in a dining car.

number dummy: A yard or car clerk; also called *number grabber*.

number grabber: See *number dummy*.

nurse 'er along: To feed fuel to a lagging locomotive.

nut buster: A machinist.

nut cracker: A roundhouse mechanic.

nuts: Small pieces of coal.

nut splitter: A mechanic or machinist.

NYPANO: The New York, Pennsylvania & Ohio Railroad.

offset-headed spike: An iron spike with a head on one side, used to fasten a rail to the ties.

off the steel: Away from the railroad.

oil can: A tank car.

oiled: Drunk.

oiler: An oil-burning locomotive. A tank car.

old girl: A steam locomotive, a term of affection.

old hand: An experienced railroader; also called *old head.*

old head: See *old hand.*

old house: A salvage warehouse. Freight on hand.

old man: A superintendent. A general manager. A conductor.

old pelican: A locomotive.

old rail: An experienced railroader.

on board: On duty.

one-lunger: A car whose coupling was pulled out of one end, a problem to the trainmen.

on the advertised: According to schedule; on time; also *on the card, on the cat hop.*

on extra board: On extra duty.

on the card: See *on the advertised.*

on the carpet: See *dance on the carpet.*

on the cat hop: See *on the advertised.*

on the cushions: In good circumstances. Riding a passenger train.

on the dirt: Off the track and on the ground; said of a derailed train.

on the grade: At a railroad construction site.

on the ground: Off the track; said of a derailed train.

on the law: To be on duty the full sixteen-hour limit set by the ICC.

on the peg: Said when the steam is at the 200-pound mark.

on the plush: To ride a passenger train.

on the rats: To steal from boxcars.

on the rip track: Said of a railroad man in the hospital. Said of a car needing repairs.

on the spot: To place a car in a designated spot. To rest or eat lunch on company time.

on the ties: Said of a derailed car or train.

on the velvet: To ride a passenger train.

OP: Short for *telegraph operator.*

open-air navigator: A hobo riding on top of a freight train.

open the gate: To switch a train onto or off a siding.

operator's fist: A type of handwriting characteristic of all telegraph operators and train dispatchers.

O.R.C.: A conductor, so called from the initials of the Order of Railway Conductors.

order board: A fixed signal regulating railroad traffic; also called *slow board, clear board,* and *red board.*

order board out: A message indicating that the agent had orders from the dispatcher.

orders: Train orders telegraphed by the dispatcher and delivered to the conductor, who then certifies them. They instruct him about stops, waits, meets, and any other movements of his train.

ornament: A stationmaster, so called from the railroader's idea that he has nothing to do in comparison with his own duties.

OS: On schedule. A train sheet. To report a train.

OS-ing: The reporting of a train by a station to the division dispatcher.

ossified: Drunk.

OT: On the track.

out: Away; said of a trainman who is at some point other than his home terminal.

outfit car: A boxcar rebuilt into a bunk car for section hands.

outlaw: To blacklist. A blacklisted striker or crew.

outshop: A new locomotive just out of the shop.

overlap: A point where two signals control the same

stretch of track.

over the hill: To go up a hill with a heavy train.

owl: A late-night passenger train. Anything pertaining to night.

Pacific-type engine: A 4-6-2 locomotive produced in 1901 by the Baldwin Locomotive Works.

paddle: A semaphore signal.

paddle the boiler: To act as engineer.

paddlewheel: A narrow-gauge locomotive with driving boxes outside the wheels.

pair of pliers: A conductor's ticket punch.

palace: A caboose.

palace car: A superior stock car.

palace sleeper: A boxcar used as living quarters, as at a road camp. A tramp's term for a boxcar.

panther sweat: Whisky.

paper car: A baggage car in which newspapers are shipped.

paper jerker: An assistant mail clerk who handles the bulky newspaper mail en route to its destination.

papers: Train orders.

paperweight: A railroad clerk. An office worker.

parlor: A caboose.

parlor boy: A flagman.

parlor brakeman: The rear brakeman of a freight train.

parlor car: An extra-fare day passenger car equipped with individual chairs.

parlor end: The rear end of a caboose.

parlor maid: A rear brakeman or flagman on a freight train. Also called *parlor man*.

parlor man: See *parlor maid*.

parlor shack: A rear brakeman.

pass: See *Annie Oakley*, *monkey money*.

passenger: One who travels by train as either a paid customer or a *deadhead*.

PASSENGER CAR

See bandwagon, baggage car, brain box, brownie box, brownie wagon, bull fighter, chair car, club car, cow wagon, cushions, day coach, diner, dining car, ding-dong, dirty car, drone cage, express car, family disturber, glass car, grass wagon, Jim Crow car, lounge car, lower berth, lower deck, money wagon, paper car, passenger coach, pay car, postal, private car, privilege car, Pullman, rubberneck car, sleeper, sleeping car, smoking car, snoozer, storage car, upper berth, varnish, varnished car, varnish wagon.

PASSENGER

See comet commuter, inside, money monkey, on the plush, on the velvet, passenger stiff, rambler, tripper.

passenger stiff: One who rides passenger trains.

pass the croaker: To be examined by the company doctor.

pasteboard: A railroad ticket.

pavilion: A caboose.

pay car: A car used to carry employees' monthly pay to the various stations in the division.

payload: A load that produces revenue for the company.

paymaster: The man whose duty it was to pay the employees their salary. He traveled with the pay car for this purpose.

peaked end: The head end of a train.

peanut roaster: A small steam engine.

pearl diver: A dishwasher in a railroad eating house.

peavine: A railroad.

peck: The twenty-minute lunch period.

peddle: To set out freight cars.

peddler: A local freight train.

pelican pond: A depression just outside the roundhouse where slush and slime are emptied from the boilers of the locomotives. The boilers are then further cleaned by blowing them out with blowoff cocks.

pencil pusher: A railroad clerk. An officer worker.

Pennsylvania: Coal.

pent house: The cupola of a caboose.

perambulator: A caboose.

persuader: A blower for locomotive fire.

petticoat: The part of the exhaust stack that guides the exhausted steam into the stack proper. If this becomes displaced, the steam returns through the flues and cuts the draft from the fire.

piano box: The switch control device.

pickle train: A train hauling bananas.

pick up: To hook on cars at a station.

pick-up: A car to be picked up.

pie book: A trainman's meal ticket; also called *pie card*.

pie card: See *pie book*.

pie-eyed: Drunk.

pifflicated: Drunk.

pig: A locomotive.

piggyback: The hauling of freight-laden motor trucks on flatcars to a destination; after delivery the trucks deliver their freight.

pig iron: A locomotive.

pig mauler: A locomotive engineer.

pigpen: A locomotive roundhouse.

pig skinner: An engineer.

pike: A railroad. A short line.

pile driver: A machine for driving down piles with a hammer; used in railroad building, especially for trestles.

pile-up: A wreck.

piling railroad: A logging railroad on trestle work

across swampy ground.

pilot: A triangular outthrust in front of the engine to push aside obstacles on the track; also called *cowcatcher.*

pilot beam: A crossbar in front of the engine to absorb the shocks and support the cowcatcher.

pilot engine: A locomotive that goes ahead of a train to make sure the way is clear.

pin: A coupler. To head for home.

pin ahead and pick up two behind: To cut off the engine, pick up three cars from a siding, put two on the train, and set the first one back on the siding.

pin for home: To go home for the day, or go off duty.

pinhead: A brakeman.

pink: A caution card or rush telegram.

pin lifter: A yard switchman.

pinner: A following switchman.

pin puller: A switchman who cuts off cars in the train yard.

piston: A closely fitting metal disk that slides back and forth within the cylinder, driven by the expansive force of steam.

piston rod: A steel rod fastened at one end to the center of a piston and at the other end to a moving block, in this manner moving the drivers.

plant: An interlocking system. A railroad detective.

plastered: Drunk.

plates: An iron shelf under a railway car.

plate wheel: An early-day wheel whose center was a

plate rather than spokes issuing from the hub.

platform car: A flatcar.

play ball: To get busy. To go to work and quit fooling around.

pliers: The conductor's ticket punch.

plow jockey: A cowboy with a cattle shipment.

plug: A "one-horse" passenger train. The throttle of an old-style locomotive. To put on air brakes in an emergency.

plug the engine: To go into reverse in making a quick stop.

plug her: To use the reverse lever as a brake in place of air.

plug puller: An engineer on a "one-horse" passenger train.

plug run: A local train.

plush: A passenger train; also called *plush haul*, *plush run*.

plush haul: See *plush*.

plush run: See *plush*.

Pocatello yardmaster: A *boomer (q.v.)*, so called because it was seemingly a custom for him to have held the tough job of night yardmaster at Pocatello, Idaho.

pod: A derail to prevent cars from running out of a siding onto the main line.

Podunk: A small, unimportant town.

pointed end: The head end of a train.

pole: To run light. To move a car on a parallel track with a pole held against the pilot beam of the locomotive.

pole pin: The superintendent of the telegraph.

pole road: In logging, a railroad track made of poles in lieu of iron rails.

pony: A switch engine.

pony express: A fast train that brought mail to a section camp.

pony trucks: The small lead wheels on a locomotive.

pop: To release the safety valve on the boiler, wasting steam and causing a loud noise.

pop car: A gasoline-powered rail car used by section men and linemen.

port: Short for *porter*, especially a passenger-train porter.

PORTER
  See bedbug, buttons, George, hop, port, redcap.

positive block: An engineer.

possum belly: A toolbox under the caboose or under a wrecking car to hold chains, buckets of dope or greasy waste used to repack hot journals, and re-railing frogs.

postal: A mail car.

pot: A locomotive.

pounder: An engineer who fails to feed or pump the engine correctly and thus makes it difficult for the fireman to keep up steam.

pound her: To work a locomotive to its full capacity.

pound their ears: To sleep.

pound the screen: To hit the spark arrester to shake loose any collected carbon so that the fire will draw better.

pound the tracks: To walk the tracks.

powder hand: A member of a dynamite crew; also called *powder monkey*.

powder monkey: See *powder hand*.

power: A locomotive.

prairie: In logging, a locomotive with a 2-6-2 wheel arrangement.

prairie-type engine: A 2-6-2 locomotive used principally in the Middle West.

private varnish: A private passenger car.

privilege car: A car on a circus train in which gambling is allowed.

pud: Short for *pick-up and delivery service*.

pull: To quit a job and leave a place; also *pull freight*.

pull a lung: To pull a drawbar to uncouple cars.

PULL A DRAWBAR
   See get a lung, lift the rivet, nip the pin, pull a lung, pull the pin, snatch the tack.

puller: A switch engine used to pull cars from one yard to another at the same terminal. The operator of an electric truck that transfers mail and baggage at a terminal.

Pullman: A railway passenger car invented and manufactured by George M. Pullman. More comfortable for day travel than the ordinary passenger car, it could be converted into bed sections for night travel. Later Pullmans were divided into roomettes, bedrooms, and compartments.

pull out a lung: To pull out a coupler by applying too much starting power. The expression arose from the fact that the air pipes were broken in addition to other damage.

pull out of service: To remove an engine or car from operation for repair or discard.

pull freight: To leave or quit a job.

pull heavy: Said of a well-loaded train.

pull the air: To set the brakes by opening the conductor's valve or angle cock.

pull the calf's tail: To pull the whistle cord.

pull the latch: To pull the throttle. To run the engine.

pull the pin: To knock off work and go home. To quit a job. To leave town. To uncouple a car by pulling up the coupling pin; derived from the old link-and-pin coupler days.

pull the white cord: To pull the emergency cord inside a car.

puncher: A telegraph operator.

punch the wind: To ride in a position exposed to the wind.

punk: A *call boy (q.v.).*

pure-food law: A crew sent out to relieve a crew that has been overtaken on the road by the sixteen-hour law.

pusher: A section boss. An extra engine at the rear of

a train to help in climbing a hill.

pusher grade: A road grade steep enough to require a helper engine at the rear.

push the shovel: To work as a fireman.

pussyfooter: A railroad policeman.

put black on white: To throw coal on a fire that is already burning at white-heat intensity.

put 'er all on: To apply the emergency brake.

put 'er on: To reduce air in the braking system.

put it in a hole: To move a car onto a side track.

put it in the big hole: To make an emergency stop.

put on the nosebag: To eat a meal.

put the Johnson bar against the running board: To get speed.

put the Johnson bar down in the corner: To get speed.

put the Johnson bar out of the cab door: To get speed.

putty: Steam.

quadruplex-type engine: An articulated compound locomotive of the Mallet type with four driving wheels.

quick-acting brake: An automatic air brake for quick responses at the rear of a train.

quick return: A fast return trip.

quill: A train whistle. To sound a whistle. In the days before whistles became standardized, each engineer had his personal technique of blowing his whistle. He could play a tune on his whistle, and some could make a whistle talk. I remember as a boy hearing a whistle on the Frisco line. The engineer's wife was named Sue. When he neared the yards, he would make his whistle say, "Oh, Sue, I'm a-comin'!" By the time he had cleaned up, checked out, and arrived home, she would have supper on the table. But it could work in reverse and give a wife's boyfriend a chance to disappear before the husband got home. Many engineers developed their own trademark with the whistle cord. (See "The Engineer's Whistle Talk" at the end of this book.)

quintuplex-type engine: An articulated compound locomotive of the Mallet type with five driving units.

R

rabbit: A switch derailer. It prevents wrecks by causing runaway trains to side-track or run off onto the prairie.

racetrack: A straight stretch of track upon which a train can go at high speed. A section of track running parallel to another company's track upon which two rival trains could hold a race. Such races broke company rules but were very enjoyable for both the trainmen and the passengers.

rack car: A railway car equipped with stakes or racks to handle pulpwood.

rack rail: A third rail between the regular track rails for locomotives with gears that engage the geared wheels of the engine to prevent slipping.

rag: A switchman.

rag waver: A flagman.

rail: A railroad employee.

rail anchor: A device that, by use of a special wrench, can be sprung into the base of a rail to grip it tightly. It is used as an anchor against a tie to prevent the rail from moving.

rail bender: A switch derailer.

rail detector car: A small car equipped to test rails for flaws.

rail fan: One who makes railroading his hobby.

rail head: The end of a railroad line.

rail hop: A train trip; also called *rail jump.*

rail jump: See *rail hop.*

RAILROAD
>   *See* TRAIN.

railroad bible: *The Official Guide to Railways.* A deck of cards.

railroader: One who does railroad work. An order for a steak in a hurry at an eating house.

railroad in a barn: A reference to the snow sheds covering tracks in western mountains. Some lines have long stretches of track covered by such sheds.

RAILROAD OFFICIAL
>   *See* brass collar, silk hat, G. M., grandpa, main pin, old man, super.

RAILROAD STATION
>   *See* depot, falling-off place, fresh-water town, jerkwater town, jumping-off place, tank town, toolbox, terminal, whistle stop.

raise water: To carry water with live steam to the cylinders.

rambler: One who rides passenger trains.

rammer: An extra engine.

rapper: An engineer who works his engine too hard.

rap the stack: To give a locomotive a wide-open throttle to make more speed.

rat: A railroad detective.

rat-crush: To rob a boxcar.

rat crusher: A locomotive.

rat hole: The fire door of an engine.

rat-hole artist: A fireman.

rat stand: A railway station.

rattle her hocks: To get speed from an engine.

rattler: A fast freight train.

rattle up: To loot a freight train while it is in motion.

rawhide: An official. An engineer running too fast when a man is stepping onto the footboard of a switch engine. An employee who is hard on the men under him. Teasing.

rawhider: An engineer who is hard on his fireman or his engine.

rawhide the fireman: To overwork the fireman.

reaction turbine: A turbine that releases steam or gas that rotates the member from which it has been ejected.

real estate: Poor-quality coal that has been mixed with dirt or slag.

rear shack: A rear brakeman.

reciprocative engine: An engine of the piston type.

red ball: A fast freight; also called *ball of fire, hotshot*.

red board: A stop signal.

redcap: A station porter. George H. Daniels, of the New York Central, originated this term in 1900.

red eye: A red signal. A red light by night is the same as a 90-degree position of the arm on a semaphore, which means "Stop." Also called *red board*. Liquor.

redhot: A train carrying fruits and potatoes from California and potatoes from Idaho. Such trains were seasonal and had the right of way over other trains.

red-light: To throw a tramp off the train.

red onion: An eating house. Sleeping quarters for railroad men.

red-order board: An order to the conductor from the agent or operator.

reef: A refrigerator car; also called *reefer*.

reefer: See *reef*.

relay: A used rail that has been taken up and relaid in a new location.

release anchors: To release hand brakes.

reload: A point where logs are transferred from one carrier to another.

REPAIR TRACK
  See graveyard, rip track.

reptile: A switchman.

required distance: The fixed distance a brakeman is required to go behind the caboose to flag a following train.

rerailer: A heavy piece of steel placed on the ties beside the rail upon which a derailed wheel can be run until it slides back onto the rail. When well oiled the wheel slides off the casting onto the rail.

rest room: A caboose.

retainer: A small valve near the brake wheel for drawing off and holding air on the cars.

ride 'em high: To place a board across the truss rods under a car and ride on it. Hobos often rode in this dangerous fashion.

ride high: To ride on top of a boxcar.

ride the blinds: To ride on the front of a baggage car.

ride the bumpers: To ride between freight cars.

ride the cushions: To work as conductor on a passenger train. A passenger.

ride the deck: To ride on top of a train, usually a freight.

ride the point: To ride in a locomotive.

ride the smoky end: To ride the engine; said of a front brakeman.

ride on velvet: To ride in a passenger car. To be in good circumstances.

RIDE A PASSENGER TRAIN
   See ride on velvet, ride the cushions, ride the plush.

ride the plush: To ride in a passenger car.

ride the point: To ride the locomotive, *point* referring to the pointed cowcatcher.

ride the rods: To *ride 'em high (q.v.).*

ride to a joint: To bring cars together for a coupling.

rift: A refrigerator car.

right-hand side: The engineer's side of the engine cab. The left-hand side is the fireman's side; when he is promoted, he is said to *set up to the right-hand side.*

right of way: The land occupied by a railroad, especially the land on which the main line travels.

ring master: A yardmaster.

ringtail: A hobo.

riprap: Heavy stones used to protect the roadbed from water erosion.

rip track: A repair track. The car-repair department. The end of the line for rolling stock.

rivet: The old-style coupling pin.

rivet buster: A boilermaker.

road bed: The bed upon which the ties, rails, and ballast of the railroad track rests.

road engine: A main-line locomotive.

road foreman: The man who reports to the superintendent on all matters and to the master mechanic on matters belonging to his department.

road hog: A large motor vehicle on a highway.

road locomotive: A main-line engine.

roadmaster: The man in charge of railroad building. A division officer responsible for keeping his division of track in good repair.

roadway: A railroad right of way with tracks and other properties.

rock: A low-grade coal.

rocker arm: An arm that receives motion at one end and conveys it to a connected part of the other.

rocking beam: A beam pivoted at some place along its length, used to convey power.

rocking chair: One who has retired on a pension.

rock rollers: A crew of men who remove rocks and other debris from the tracks.

rods: One of the underbracings of a railway car.

rod engine: A locomotive in which the power is transmitted to the wheels from the cylinders by a main rod and side rods.

rodman: One who rides the rods. A member of the surveying crew.

roll 'em: To get speed.

roll their own: Said of a railroad company that built its own locomotives instead of purchasing them from outside manufacturers.

rolling outhouse: In logging, a cabin placed on a flatcar behind the engine.

rolling stock: The wheeled cars owned by a railroad. A doughnut.

roofed: Caught in close clearance.

roofer: One who rides the roofs of trains.

roof garden: A Mallet-type locomotive or any helper engine used on a mountain job.

rooster: A long bar used to couple cars, one of which was a link-and-pin and the other a knuckler coupler. The rooster is no longer used because the link-and-pin coupler is no longer in existence.

rotary plow: A large revolving fan mounted at the front of a railway car to throw snow from the track during mountain winters.

rotate the bulletin board: To rotate the job-assignment board. The board is a six-sided form mounted on a pivot. By rotating it, one can read the new job assignments and other information.

roughneck: A brakeman.

roundhouse: A circular building housing idle loco-motives and those needing repair. On the outside front is a turntable to move them in and out on the proper track.

ROUNDHOUSE
  See barnhouse, madhouse, pigpen, roundhouse.

ROUNDHOUSE MECHANIC
  See chambermaid, kettle mender, nut splitter, nut buster, nut cracker.

rounds: A member of an extra train crew.

round trip: A journey to a certain place and return, usually over the same route.

rubberneck car: An observation car.

Rule G: A rule adopted by the Association of American Railroads prohibiting drinking or use of narcotics by railroad employees. It is a club used by the railroad companies to make railroads safer. A man discharged for breaking this rule finds it very difficult to get another job as a railroader.

run: The train to which an employee is assigned. It is his regular route, usually from one division to another.

run-around: A temporary track built beside the main line to move a train past an obstruction. Hence a man who is not notified when it is his turn to work is said to have been given the *run-around*. He is entitled to claim pay for the missed work.

run-fast: Engine lubricating oil.

run-in: A collision.

run light: To run an engine on the track without cars.

runner: A locomotive engineer.

running gear: The gear that propels the locomotive.

run on smoke orders: To run a train from one station or siding to another without orders from the dispatcher. Each engineer looked out for the smoke of another train. It was a dangerous way to run a railroad and is now obsolete.

runt: A dwarf signal.

rust: A track that has not been used for some time.

rust eater: A track layer.

rustle the bums: To search a freight train for hobos. The search gave the brakemen a chance to collect transportation money from the hobos, usually a dollar a division.

rust pile: An old, worn-out locomotive.

rusty rail: An old hand at railroading.

sacred cow: A helper locomotive on a mountain run. Also called *sacred ox*.

sacred ox: See *sacred cow*.

saddle: The first step of a freight car under the lowest grab iron.

saddle tank: A water tank over the locomotive boiler. It also provided weight over the driver wheels.

safety valve: A valve on the boiler to let the steam escape when it reached a certain pressure.

sag: The bottom of a down grade.

sailor: A streamlined train.

saloon: A caboose.

sand dome: A bin straddling the boiler top of the locomotive, filled with sand that was used to sand the track for better traction.

sandhog: A laborer who works in a caisson tunneling under a river or boring a railroad tunnel.

SAP: The San Antonio and Arkansas Pass Railroad. A brake club.

S.A.P.: Short for *soon as possible,* a sign on a time board.

sap up some binders: To set hand brakes.

saturated steam: Steam containing liquid droplets.

savages: One of a gang of workmen composed of tramps with a tramp foreman.

sawbones: A company doctor.

saw by: A method of passing a train on a single track used when the siding is too short to hold an entire train. It is a tedious and complicated operation.

saw her off: To cut off the locomotive from a train.

scab: A nonunion worker. A car not equipped with an automatic air system.

scalper: A person who sells tickets at reduced rates.

schedule: A timetable of the runs of a railroad.

scissorbill: A yard or road brakeman. A beginner in railroading; not a complimentary term.

scoop: A fireman's shovel. The step on the front and rear ends of a switch engine.

scoot: A shuttle train.

scorch the iron: To run a train at high speed.

scrap pile: A worn-out engine that is still in service.

scrap track: See *rip track.*

SD: Short for *signal displayed.*

seashore: Sand used from the *sand dome (q.v.).* Coal mixed with sand.

seat hog: A passenger using more than one seat in a

passenger car or station waiting room while others are forced to stand.

Seattle car: A railroad log car on which the pair of trucks are connected by one stout center sill. Also called *skeleton car.*

secret works: Automatic brakes. The draft timbers and drawbar of a car pulled out by force.

section: A laborer on a section gang.

section boss: The foreman of a section gang.

SECTION BOSS
>*See* ballet dancer, gaffer, gang pusher, herder, king snipe, pusher, section boss, snipe king, warden.

section gang: A crew of track workers employed to keep a certain section of track in good condition. They also weed the right of way, replace rotted ties, reballast, raise the track if necessary, fill in sags, and resurface. They rest while a train passes.

SECTION GANG
>*See* chain gang, checkerboard crew, dino, extra gang, gandy dancer, gandy gang, jerry, snipe, rock roller, terrier, track hand.

section-indicator post: A post numbered to indicate the end of the section of a particular foreman.

SECTION MAN
>*See* crumb boss, dino, dirt dauber, dirt hider, donkey, extra gang, floating gang, gaffer, galloping goose, gang pusher, gandy dancer, gandy gang, grave digger, herder, king snipe, lizard scorcher, mucker, pusher, rust eater, sandhog, section gang, section hand, snipe,

snipe king, speeder, spic, spotboard, storm king, straw boss, track hand, warden, weeder.

semaphore: An apparatus for visual signaling.

seniority: The right of passenger trains over freights and of express trains over locals. The right of way in one direction on a single-track line. The length of service of an employee.

seniority grabber: A railroad worker who is up for promotion when another worker with more seniority dies, is fired, or resigns.

separation: The sorting of mail sacks and parcels before transfer to trucks.

serpent: A switchman, so called because of the serpentine letter *S* on his Switchman's Union membership pin.

service application: A gradual reduction in speed, as contrasted with an emergency stop.

service position: A position of the brake valve that starts the air pumps that charge the train line.

set out: To sidetrack.

set-out: Cars left on a siding.

set up: To load a baggage car with mail and parcels following an advance plan to make it easier for fast unloading at the various stations along the route.

setup: A group of hand trucks in formation beside the door of the baggage and mail cars to make it easier to separate the mail being unloaded.

set up to the right-hand side: To be promoted from fireman to engineer.

shack: A brakeman at the rear of a train. A caboose.

shack house: A caboose.

shack's master: A freight conductor.

shack stinger: A brakeman.

shag: A brakeman.

shake: To switch in a switch yard. Also *shake 'em out, shake 'em up.*

shake the lines over the iron mule: To run a *donkey (q.v.).*

shake the train: To put on the air brakes in an emergency.

shanty: A caboose.

sharp end: The head end of a train.

Shay-type engine: A logging locomotive named for its inventor, Ephraim Shay, in 1880. The Shay was a geared engine, and connected to the crankshaft was a line shaft that carried the power to all the axles. The flexible linkage and bevel gears connected the longitudinal crankshaft and the wheels of two trucks. The boiler was set left of center, giving it a lopsided appearance. Also called *sidewinder.*

shelter house: A caboose; a term especially used by logging railroads.

shelter wagon: A caboose.

shifter: A switch engine.

shine: To go on duty.

shiner: The brakeman's or switchman's lantern.

shining time: Starting time; the time at which one reports for work.

shiny pants: A railway clerk.

shoe: A crescent of metal that drags against the tread of a wheel when the brake is applied, thus stopping its turning.

shoofly: A temporary track built around an obstacle such as a wreck or a flooded-out place.

shoot the works: To make an emergency stop.

short: A car set out between stations.

short call: A call to a crew for less than half an hour's work.

short-fire: To fail to throw coal far enough into the firebox.

short-flag: In signaling, to fail to go far enough behind the train to protect it properly.

short-line: To operate trains over a comparatively short distance.

short load: A car consigned to a point between division points and set out on a siding at the destination; also called *short.*

short of cars: Unemployed.

short tail: A nonunion man.

short-time: To be late on the job; said of a trainman late on his route.

short-time crew: A crew working overtime, not yet affected by the sixteen-hour law.

shoulder: See *axle offset.*

SHOVEL
> *See* banjo, diamond pusher, idiot stick, tool of ignorance, ukelele.

show the white feather: To release steam from the safety valve.

shuffle: To switch cars.

shuffle the deck: To switch cars onto *house tracks (q.v.)* at every station on the run.

shunting boiler: A switch engine.

shuttle train: A train that travels back and forth on frequent runs.

side-door Pullman: A boxcar used by tramps stealing a ride.

side rod: A loading foreman. An executive assistant. A steel rod connecting the crank pins of any two adjoining driving wheels on the same side of the locomotive.

sideswipe: A collision at a switch when cars or engines strike each other a glancing blow.

side tank: An engine on which the tanks are carried on either side of the boiler.

side track: A railway siding.

SIDE-TRACK
> *See* go in the hole, go on a farm, head in, put in a hole, set out.

side-wheeler: A low-geared engine for heavy hauling.

sidewinder: A Shay-geared engine.

signal man: One who signals or works with signals.

silent eye: A railroad detective.

silk glove: A passenger conductor.

silk hat: A railroad official.

silver-dollar route: A railroad on which the crew charges hobos a dollar a division.

simple articulated locomotive: A locomotive on which all cylinders receive steam at full boiler pressure; the opposite of a *compound articulated locomotive (q.v.)*.

single-acting piston: A piston that exerts its thrust in one direction only.

single stick: A single camshaft on a diesel engine.

singletree: A coupling.

sing on the pops: To release a wisp of steam from the safety valve.

single iron: Single track.

skate: A shoe placed on a rail in the *hump yard (q.v.)* to stop cars with defective brakes.

skeleton car: A car on which the trucks are held together by a center beam, but having no deck; used for hauling logs.

skin your eye: An engineer's warning to his fireman when approaching a curve.

skipper: A conductor.

skip the cinders: To walk the track.

skip the ties: To walk the track.

skunk: See *call boy*.

skyrocket: A red-hot cinder from the smokestack.

slack: To back the engine far enough to relieve the tension on the couplers between the tender and the first car. Poor coal.

slaughter house: A railroad yard, so called because so many switchmen were killed there.

slave driver: A yardmaster. A *rawhider (q.v.)*.

sleep: To give sleeping accommodations to someone.

sleeper: A Pullman sleeping car. An unnoticed piece of mail left in the mail car.

sleep in: To go back to sleep after being called for duty.

SLEEPING CAR
  See sleeper, sleeping car, snoozer.

slide valve: A valve that admits steam into and exhausts it from a cylinder.

sliding axle: See *lateral-play axle*.

slim gauge: A train or track less than 4 feet, 8½ inches wide.

sling Morse: To operate a telegraph.

smoke agent: See *smoke*.

smokebox: The portion of the boiler ahead of the water section.

smoke boy: A fireman who is working on an engine making a lot of smoke.

smoker: A railroad car or compartment in which smoking is allowed.

smoking car: A *smoker (q.v.)*.

smoke 'em: To move a train from one station to another without orders, watching for the smoke of an approaching train. See *smoke orders*.

smoke orders: The early-day practice of moving a train from one station to another without orders, the enginemen watching for the smoke of an approaching train on the same track. Also called *smoke signals.*

smoke signals: See *smoke orders.*

smokestack: A steel chimney attached to the upper part of the smokebox for the discharge of smoke and gases.

smokolotive: A locomotive.

slip: See *slip car.*

slip car: A carload of bananas; also called *slip.*

slip down: To spin the engine's drivers because of slick rails.

slough: To throw a tramp off a train.

slow board: A fixed signal regulating traffic.

slug: A heavy fire in the locomotive firebox. To supply fuel too rapidly.

slug: A shipment of magazines and other bags of mail weighing about one hundred pounds.

smart aleck: A passenger conductor.

smasher: A baggageman.

smash up: To have a wreck.

smoke: A fireman; also called *smoke agent.*

smoky end: The head end of a train.

smooth: A ten-cent tip.

snake: A switchman, so called from the serpentine letter *S* on his membership pin. Also called *reptile, serpent.*

snake a stiff: To allow a tramp to ride the train.

snakehead: A rail that has come loose from the ties and pierced the floor of a car.

snap: To push or pull a train up a hill with an extra engine.

snapper: An engine that pushes or pulls with another.

snatch the tack: To uncouple or pull a drawbar. To stop.

snipe: A track laborer.

snipe king: A section boss.

snoozer: A Pullman car.

snow dodger: A winter tourist in the South. Also called *snow flyer*.

snow flyer: See *snow dodger*.

snow plow: A rotary plow fastened to the front end of a locomotive to remove snow from the tracks.

snow shed: A shelter built over the track to protect against snow slides.

snow train: A special passenger train traveling to a winter-sports region. A train that plows snow off the tracks.

snozzled: Drunk.

snuff dipper: An early-day engine that burned snuff-colored lignite coal.

soak: A saturated locomotive. See *saturated steam*.

soda jerker: A fireman.

soft belly: A wood-frame railroad car.

soft coaler: A railroad that hauls bituminous coal.

soft-diamond special: A coal train.

soft plug: A fusible plug in the crown sheet of the engine that drops when the water falls below the top of the sheet.

solid car: A storage car filled with mail and parcels.

solid track: A track full of cars.

soup: Water.

soup ticket: The superintendent's ticket that reports the official arrival and departure times of a train.

sowbelly: A steel car. A coal car with a drop bottom and bulging sides; also called *whale belly*.

spar: A pole used to shove cars into the clear when switching.

sparks: A telegraph operator. The flashes from a hot engine.

spark arrester: A device for preventing cinders from escaping from the engine smokestack. Also called *spark cap*.

spark cap: See *spark arrester*.

SPEED
> *See* ball of fire, ball the jack, ballast scorcher, barrel, bat the stack off her, beat her on the back, beat the throttle with a stick, cannonball express, carry the mail, drop her in the corner, fan, fast freight, flip, fog, have it up against the brass, highball, high-tail, hit the ball, lightning express, roll 'em, walk the dog, wheel, wheel the barries, widen on her.

speeder: A gasoline-powered railroad car used by section men. A caboose.

speed gauger: An engineer.

speedy: A *call boy (q.v.)*.

spic: A section man, so called especially in the Southwest, where many section men were Mexican.

spike a torch: To throw a *fusee (q.v.)* in such a way that it would stick into a tie.

spike driver: A machine similar to the hammer driven by air compressors and used in latter-day railroad building instead of manpower.

spiker: A man who drove the spikes when laying rails.

spill: A railroad station.

spot: To place a car in a designated place. To sleep, rest, or take a lunch period on company time. Time at the end of the line or between shifts.

spot a car: To place a car in position for loading or unloading.

spot board: A guide used by section men when ballasting a track to produce an even roadbed.

spotter: A company spy hired to check on employees.

squeezer: A car-retarding system used in some railroad yards.

squirrel: To climb up the side of a car.

squirrel a car: To climb onto cars to set hand brakes.

squirt: The water injector on an engine.

stab: To delay or cause a loss of time.

stack: Short for *smokestack*.

stack buster: An engineer who fails to *hook 'er up (q.v.)*.

stack of reds: A succession of red lights.

stack of rust: An engine that has seen better days.

stack up: To have a wreck.

staff of ignorance: The brake club used by brakemen.

stagger soup: Whisky.

stake: A pole used in switching; a cut of cars was shoved with a pole attached to the car immediately behind the engine. The money a *boomer (q.v.)* saved on the job to use for food after he quit to look for another job.

stake-driver: Any engineering department man, usually a member of the surveying crew.

stall: A space separated by revolving steel posts to sort and store mail and parcels consigned to certain destinations.

standard gauge: A railroad track and engine-wheel width of 4 feet, 8½ inches.

stargazer: A brakeman who fails to see signals.

start the hind end first: To jerk a train into sudden motion.

starvation diet: A fixed signal regulating railroad traffic.

stationmaster: The man in charge of a railroad station.

STATION
> *See* depot, falling-off place, fresh-water town, jerkwater, jumping-off place, mudhole, ornament, rat stand, spill, stopping-off place, tank town, teapot, terminal, toolbox, waiting room, whistle stop, wise guy.

station track: See *house track*.

steam: Fog.

steam-brake: To reverse the valve gear to slow engine speed. This means of braking was risky because of the danger of blowing out the cylinder heads and was used only in an emergency.

steam dome: A container on top of the engine boiler for in which steam accumulates.

steam-heat man: A passenger trainman.

steam horse: A locomotive.

steam pump: See *injector*.

steam stop: A train stop in which steam power is used, applying the brakes on the cars but not on the engine.

steam wagon: A locomotive.

steam-wagon road: A railroad.

steel boy: A steel car.

steel gang: A crew of men who lay rails.

steel man: A track layer.

stem: The track or right of way.

stem-winder: A climax-type geared locomotive.

Stephenson gear: A valve gear with which an engineer could run an engine backward or forward and regulate the period during which steam was admitted into the cylinder.

stewed: Drunk.

stick: A staff used on certain stretches of track to control the block.

stiff buggy: A four-wheel truck specially designed for

use in transferring coffins and boxes at a station.

stinger: A brakeman; probably derived from the brakeman's custom of applying his brake club to the feet of a sleeping hobo. A fast train.

stink buggy: A gasoline bus.

stinker: A hotbox.

stirrup: The first step on a freight car, under the lower grab iron.

stock: See *stock car*.

stock car: A slatted car for hauling stock, with mangers on the sides for feeding; also called *stock*, *stocker*.

stocker: See *stock car*.

stockholder: Any employee who looks out for the company's interest.

stock pen: The stationyard office. The pens that hold stock to be shipped.

stock run: See *stock train*.

stock train: A train of cattle on the way to market; also called *stock run*.

stoker: A device for adding fuel to the firebox. A fireman.

stoke the hay burner: To add fuel to the firebox.

stop gun: A track torpedo.

stop over: To stop at some point before proceeding on a journey.

stopover: A stopping-off place on a journey.

stopping-off place: A small station or town.

stopper puller: A member of the crew that follows the engine in switching.

storage car: A baggage car. Any car used during rush periods to ship mail sacks to be transferred to certain terminals for rerouting by other trains to other destinations.

storm curtain: A heavy canvas curtain hanging in the gangway of the engine to protect the engine crew in the winter.

storm king: A carefully selected man who works in mountain divisions. He is dedicated to battling the winter storms to get the trains through and considers it an honor to be selected for the work.

stovepipe: Gossip.

STOWAWAY
> *See* blind baggage, flipper, jumper, train chaser, train crasher.

straight-air brake: See *atmospheric brake.*

straight spout: An oil can with a special type of pipe connection.

straight ticket: A one-way railway ticket.

strap iron: A flat iron bar mounted on a wooden stringer, sometimes used as a running rail.

strawberry patch: The rear end of a caboose at night, so called because of its red light. A railroad yard studded with red lights.

straw boss: The foreman of a small gang of section men.

straw-hat boy: A railroader who works only in pleasant weather.

steak of rust: A little-used or discontinued track.

streamliner: A fast train.

STREAMLINE TRAIN
  See caterpillar, sailor, streamliner, tin lizard.

stretch 'er out: To take the slack out of couplings and drawbars.

string: A line of cars coupled together. A telegraph wire.

stringer: A brakeman.

string of boxes: A train of boxcars.

string of flats: A train of flatcars. Hot cakes.

string of varnish: A passenger train composed of the highly varnished wooden coaches used before modern steel cars.

stroke: An interchanging movement, such as that of a piston rod.

struggle for life: Life in a railroad boardinghouse.

stub: A train that takes over part of the schedule of another train. A dead-end spur of a railroad.

stub switch: A switch having the track rails cut off squarely and with the switch rails butt end-to-end with the lead rails.

student: A learner in telegraph, train, or engine service. An apprentice.

student smoke agent: An apprentice fireman; also called *student tallow pot, stude tallow.*

student tallow pot: See *student smoke agent.*

stude tallow: See *student smoke agent.*

suck it by: To make a *flying switch (q.v.).*

sugar: Sand.

sunflower stack: A wide-mouthed smokestack.

sun parlor: The cupola of a caboose.

supe: The *consist (q.v.)* of a train.

super: Short for *superintendent.*

superheated steam: Steam directed through auxiliary coils in the flues to increase its temperature.

superheater: A heater that produces *superheated steam (q.v.).*

supply train: A train that gathers scrap and delivers supplies to all points on the division, usually in a three-month period.

Swede car: In early-day railroad construction, a hand-pushed car used for dumping fill dirt along the grade.

swellhead: An engineer. A conductor.

swing brakeman: The brakeman serving the middle of the train. He is in charge of setting out cars and braking the section between those handled by the head and parlor brakemen. Also called *swing.*

swing a bug: To make a good job of braking.

swing down on: To give a stop signal.

swing man: An extra brakeman who works out on one train and comes back on another, thus allowing the legal limit of a train to be increased. Speed was demanded as part of his day's work, and it took a toll of life and limb.

switch: A device made of two movable rails with connections that work to turn an engine or train from one track to another. A railroad siding. To switch cars.

SWITCH

>See chisel, drop a car, drum, fly in, kick, shake, shake 'em out, shuffle, shuffle the deck.

switchback: A zigzag railroad track built across a hill too steep for direct ascent.

switch engine: An engine used exclusively to switch cars in a switch yard; also called *switcher*.

switcher: See *switch engine*.

switch inspector: A man expert in the installation and upkeep of the *switch (q.v.)*.

switch list: The menu of a railroad eating house.

switchman: A worker who operates a *switch (q.v.)*, either manually or electrically.

SWITCHMAN

>See bend the iron, bend the rails, bend the rust, bug slinger, cherry picker, chisel, cinder cruncher, close the gate, clown, club wonder, dolly flapper, drop, dropper, fixed man, fly in, flying switch, footboard yardmaster, gate, herd the calliope, highball the switch, high daddy, janney, jawbone shack, jerk-by, jockey, lunar white, open the gate, ping-pong, rag, rag waver, serpent, shake 'em out, shake 'em up, shuffle the deck, snake, suck it by, switch, switch monkey, switch yard, tower man, work in the field, yard geese.

switch monkey: A *switchman (q.v.)*.

switch run: A combination switch and freight train.

switch shanty: A small building in which switchmen keep their lanterns and seek shelter in bad weather.

switch yard: A yard in which railroad cars are switched from one track to another in making up trains.

tack: A coupling pin.

tail-ender: A rear-end collision.

tail over her back: Said of an engine under a full head of steam, with a plume of steam coming from her safety valve.

tail sign: The illuminated name on the observation car.

take a bath: To take water at a tank where the spout is not adjusted properly or is too short.

take a spout of juice: To take water.

take it by the neck: To pull a *drag (q.v.)* up a steep grade.

take the rubbers out of 'em: To disconnect the air hoses on a train.

take the slack: To reverse the engine before starting forward.

take to the cinders: To walk the track. To quit a job.

TAKE WATER
> *See* bathe, jerk a drink, jerk soup, take a bath, take a spout of juice.

take minutes: To stop for lunch.

talent trunks: The baggage of touring actors and actresses.

tallow dip: A fireman.

tallow pot: A fireman, so called because he used tallow to oil the valves and shine the engine. An engine lubricated with tallow.

tandem compound-type engine: A locomotive having on each side a high- and a low-pressure cylinder set end to end and with the pistons mounted on one rod.

tangent track: The portion of a track immediately adjacent to a curve.

tank: A locomotive tender.

TANK CAR
> *See* can, oiler, tanker.

tanked: Drunk.

tank engine: A locomotive that carried the water and fuel tanks over the drivers rather than in a tender.

tanker: A car used for hauling oil, chemicals, milk, and other liquids.

tank town: A small station or town.

tank-type engine: See *tank engine*.

target: A semaphore signal.

tar pot: A fireman. A locomotive.

teakettle: A small locomotive, especially an old, leaky one.

tease the brute: To follow the engine.

teddy: The sixteen-hour law.

TELEGRAPHER
> *See* brass pounder, bug, buzzer, fist, flimsy, flipping tissues, flopping tissues, ham, key, lid, lightning slinger, OP, operator's fist, orders, pink, pole pin, puncher, sling Morse, sparks, thirty, wire tapper.

telltale: A series of dangling ropes placed shortly before a train approached a low bridge or the entrance to a tunnel to warn any rider on top of a boxcar to duck or get his head smashed. In logging, a tall stick placed vertically on the end of the last log car; its presence signified that the train was intact.

tender: A vehicle attached behind the locomotive for carrying fuel and water for the engine.

ten-wheeler: A locomotive with four wheels on the pony truck and six drivers.

terminal: A city or town at the end of a railway line. A train station that serves as a junction with other lines. A town at the end of a division in which there are yards and other facilities. A railway post-office unit in which mail is sorted and rerouted to its destination.

terminal load: A shipment of mail consigned to a railway post-office terminal office for sorting and reshipment.

terrier: A section hand.

Texas-type engine: A large 2-10-4 locomotive first used by the Texas and Pacific Railroad in 1926.

thin skin: A fireman.

third rail: A rail added to a track on curves to prevent derailment. A metal rail carrying the current to an electric locomotive.

thirty: A telegrapher's signal at the end of a message meaning "That's all."

thirty days and thirty brownies: A fine imposed for an infraction of a rule: thirty days without pay and thirty demerits.

thirty-one order: A train order that must be signed, making it necessary for the train to come to a stop to receive it.

thousand-miler shirt: A blue percale or black sateen shirt worn by railroad workers because it supposedly did not show dirt after being worn a thousand miles.

three-bagger: A train pulled or pushed by three engines.

three-cylinder compound-type engine: A locomotive with a third cylinder that receives steam from two cylinders outside the frames or feeds its own exhaust into them.

throat: A fan-shaped convergence of tracks at the entrance to a tunnel.

throttle: The equipment that controls the proper amount of steam admitted into the cylinders.

throttle artist: An engineer.

throttle fever: Ambition for promotion; said of a fireman eager to become an engineer.

throttle jerker: An engineer.

throttle puller: An engineer.

throttle valve: A valve used to regulate the supply of steam from the boiler to the cylinders.

throw away the diamonds: To miss the fire door or spill coal when shoveling it into the firebox.

throw her into the big hole: To make an emergency stop.

thumb buster: A mechanic.

thumbs up: A signal for the engine man to take a rest while the train is on a siding.

ticker: A pocket watch.

ticket: A document or certificate, usually a small printed cardboard, showing that a fare fee has been paid. The underbracing of a railway car.

TICKET
> *See* commutation ticket, ducat, pasteboard, ticket agent, ticket chopper, ticket office, ticket punch, ticket scalper, ticket snatcher, transportation, straight ticket.

ticket agent: The man in the station or downtown office who sells tickets to passengers.

ticket chopper: A ticket-canceling box.

ticket office: The station office where railroad tickets are sold.

ticket punch: A pair of pliers.

ticket scalper: A man who buys and sells overpriced tickets for a quick profit.

ticket snatcher: A passenger conductor.

tie: One of the wooden supports to which the rails are fastened to keep them in line and form a solid rest. To couple cars.

tied: In railroad construction, an expression meaning that ties have been placed ready for laying the track.

tie down: See *tie 'em down.*

tie 'em down: To set hand brakes on a car before leaving it on a siding or spur.

tie 'em together: To couple cars.

tie on: To couple cars.

tie on the rubber: To couple the air hose.

tie pass: A tramp's fictitious "permit" to walk the ties.

tier: A pile of mail stacked the full width at each end of a car.

ties: A railroad right of way as used by tramps.

tie the train down: To set hand brakes.

tie the wind: To fasten the air hose.

tie up: To stop for a rest or meal. The end of a run, when the crew goes off duty.

time card: A schedule of train movements. An official railroad publication giving the schedule of all trains in a division.

time-card train: A fast train.

timepiece: A timekeeper. A watch.

timetable: A folding-sheet schedule. A table of arrival and departure times of the trains of a certain railroad and its connections with other roads.

Timkenized: Equipped with Timken roller bearings.

ting-a-ling: A small engine with a tinny bell.

tin hat: A railroad official.

tinkerer: A repairman.

tin lizard: A streamlined train.

tin star: A railroad detective.

TIP

> *See* bird, Boston quarter, lamb's tongue, nigger tip, smooth, turkey.

tissues: A train order; see *flimsy*.

T.M.: Short for *trainmaster (q.v.)*.

toad: A derailing device.

toepath: The running board on a locomotive. The catwalk on top of a boxcar. The part of a railway embankment between the end of the ties and the shoulders of the fill.

tonk: A car repairman.

tonnage hound: Any railroad official who insists on longer and heavier trains than the engine's power can pull.

tonnage rating: The weight limit that certain classes of locomotives could pull.

tonsil paint: Whisky.

toolbox: A small station or town.

tool of ignorance: A coal shovel.

toothpick: A railroad tie.

top dresser drawer: The upper bunk in a caboose.

top off the tank: To fill the water tank.

torpedo: A flare signal shaped like a small pillbox with two lead strips attached for fastening it to the rail, one to bend around the rail to keep it from being jarred off and the other to lie along the rail.

torpedoes: Beans.

tough road: A railroad hostile to tramps.

tour: A work shift.

tower buff: A rail fan who ignores the "Keep Out" signs on switch towers and other structures.

tower man: A man in the switching tower who works the switches from the engineer's whistle signals.

towpath: See *toepath*.

trackage: Lines of railway tracks. The privilege of using the tracks of other roads.

track hand: A section hand.

track illuminator: The original "headlight," first used in 1831. It was a flatcar covered with sand upon which was placed a metal box filled with burning pine knots.

track layer: A track-laying vehicle. A man employed to lay rails.

track stiff: A tramp who walked along the track.

track walker: A man hired to walk over a section of track and inspect it for flaws.

traction increaser: An apparatus for conveying part of the weight of the fuel car from one of its trucks to the driving wheels to increase traction when starting.

tractive force: The degree of effort employed by a locomotive in turning the wheels.

trade water for steam: To close the injector often to gain steam.

trailer: A flatcar pushed ahead of the engine to couple onto other cars that are on a section of track unfit for a heavy locomotive.

trailerman: A rear brakeman.

trailer truck: A truck under the firebox and behind the driving wheels of the locomotive to help carry the weight of the engine.

train: A line of railway cars. To transport by train.

TRAIN

> *See* accommodation train, big boy, black one, black snake, bobtail bounce, bumsick train, butter-and-egg run, caboose bounce, caboose hop, cannonball express, caterpillar, combination train, crack train, croppy, dangler, dicer, donkey, doubleheader, drag, drunkard, extra, fast freight, flyer, flying squadron, freighter, gravy train, greenball freight, green carrier, hotshot, hotshot freight, humpback job, immigrant train, jerkwater, lightning express, limited, liner, lying dead, merchandise peddler, mixed train, Modoc, night owl, peddler, pickle train, plug, plug run, plush, rattler, red ball, sailor scoot, slip, snow train, soft-diamond special, stock run, stock train, streamliner, string of varnish, supply train, three-bagger, time-card train, tin lizard, traveling switch engine, varnish job, varnish run.

train bull: A railroad detective.

train captain: An early-day title for a conductor.

train chaser: A stowaway.

train crasher: A stowaway.

train detainer: A train dispatcher.

train dick: A railroad detective.

train dispatcher: A man who directs the action of trains of a certain division and cooperates with other dispatchers in their movement from his division to others.

train line: One of the pipes that carry compressed air to operate the brakes.

train load: The capacity of a freight or passenger train.

trainman: A member of a train crew supervised by a conductor.

trainmaster: The man responsible for keeping correct schedules, the departure of trains, and the operation of the switch yards.

TRAIN ORDER
See flimsy, flip tissues, fumble the hoop, papers, lap order, pink, tissue.

tramp: A hobo. A slow freight train. An engine in poor condition used only in an emergency.

trampified: An expression describing how a *boomer* *(q.v.)* looks after a long period without work.

tramp ticket: A grooved board made to fit over the rods of a freight car upon which hobos rode.

transfer table: A table with a single track that is moved back and forth to align with other parallel tracks, used to transfer a locomotive from one track to another.

transportation: A railroad ticket.

trap: A storage box that receives sand from the sand dome and releases it to the rails below.

trapeze artist: One who rode the rods; a hobo, so called because of the dangerous climbs he made onto moving trains.

travel: Transportation of perishable produce.

traveling card: A postcard from a railroad brother to a man searching for a job. An empty slip bill; see *slip*.

traveling grunt: A road engine foreman. A traveling engineer.

traveling man: An engine man not assigned to a regular run.

traveling switch engine: A local freight engine.

travel on a tie pass: To walk the track.

treasure chest: A caboose.

trespasser: A tramp who walks along the railroad track.

trestle: A braced framework of timbers, piles, or steelwork for carrying a train over a depression, chasm, or river.

trick: A work or duty shift.

trimmer: A hump-yard engine used to shove misdirected cars into the clear.

trip: A shift of duty from one terminal to another and return.

triple valve: An apparatus connected to the brake pipe, the auxiliary, and the brake cylinder to regulate the intake and exhaust of the compressed air in the brake system.

triplex-type engine: An articulated compound locomotive of the Mallet type having three driving units, one of which is beneath the tender.

tripper: A passenger on a passenger train.

troubleshooter: A man responsible for the maintenance of the right of way.

truck: A carriage with one or more pairs of wheels and springs that swivel to guide one end of a car or locomotive as it turns sharp curves.

trumpet stack: A stack shaped like a long, inverted cone.

try the air: To inspect the brake equipment.

T.T.: Short for *train tourists*.

turkey: A fifty-cent tip.

turn him in: To report a person for bad conduct or theft.

turn in: To go to bed.

turn out: A railroad siding.

turntable: A platform with a track for turning wheeled vehicles. It has a steel girder supported on bearings and is long enough to hold a locomotive. Under the outer edges are wheels to carry part of the weight. In the old days it was turned by hand, but in modern times it is worked by compressed air or an electric motor.

two-check man: An employee who informs against another worker.

two-gun hogger: An engineer who used both water injectors, thus making it hard for his fireman to keep up steam.

two pipes of lake shore: The sand in the engine sand dome.

two-wheeler: A two-wheeled hand truck for transferring baggage and mail at a station.

ukelele: A short-handled scoop or shovel.

Uncle Sam: The railway post-office clerk.

undercarriage: The frame and running gear of a locomotive.

undercover man: A railroad detective hired to spy on workmen.

underground hog: The chief engineer.

under the flag: Under a work certificate; said of a *boomer (q.v.)* who works under someone else's letter or certificate.

under the pops: The maximum steam pressure possible without unseating the safety valves.

under the table: Said of a telegraph operator who is receiving messages faster than he can transcribe them.

unload: To go off duty. To get off a train hurriedly. To jump off a runaway train.

upper berth: The top berth in a sleeping car. The top of a car. Also called *upper deck.*

upper deck: See *upper berth.*

valve: A mechanical device with a movable lid that allows or prevents the passage of steam.

valve gear: An apparatus that directs steam in or out of the cylinders, allowing a locomotive to run backward or forward.

valve rod: A steel rod that transfers the motion of an eccentric rod to a valve.

van: A caboose.

vapor jack: A piston-and-cylinder apparatus on a locomotive to take some of the weight from the fore and aft trucks and apply it to the drivers to improve traction at starting and on grades.

varnish: A wooden passenger car, so called because they were lacquered to a shine.

varnished boxes: A passenger train made up of varnished wooden coaches.

varnished car: A wooden passenger car.

varnished wagon: A wooden passenger car.

varnish job: A passenger train made up of wooden coaches; also called *varnish run, varnish shot.*

varnish run: See *varnish job*.

varnish shot: See *varnish job*.

Vaseline: Oil.

Vauclain compound-type engine: A locomotive with high- and low-pressure cylinders, one above the other, on each side, with piston rods stroking a single main rod.

vent: A ventilated refrigerator car.

virgin: A letter to be postmarked.

Wabash: A big fire in the locomotive firebox. To hit a car going into an adjacent switch. To slow for a stop signal instead of coming to a complete stop, as officially ruled, thus saving the engineer several minutes' time.

wagon: A railway car.

waiting room: A room in a railway station for people waiting for a train.

walking beam: A counterbalanced lever.

walking Dudley: A unique type of steam locomotive known as the Fouts grip wheel, used in logging in the Northwest. Its power is furnished by a vertical boiler mounted on a small car which propels itself by means of a road cable extending the length of the road.

walk the dog: To run a freight train so fast that the cars sway from side to side.

walk the ties: To walk the track.

WALK THE TRACK
> *See* beat the trains, count the ties, hit the cinders, hit the cinder trail, pound the tracks, skip

the cinders skit the ties, take to the cinders, tie pass, travel on a tie pass, walk the ties.

walk up against the gun: To ascend a steep grade with the injector on.

Wall Street notch: The forward corner of the reverse lever quadrant in the engine cab, so called because it was said that the engine paid dividends when it worked this way with heavy loads.

Walschaerts: A locomotive driving gear designed by Egide Walschaerts, a Belgian, in 1900. It was the first valve gear placed outside the wheels for convenience in servicing.

wanigan car: The timekeeper's headquarters. The office car of a railroad camp.

warden: A section boss.

Ward's catcher: A large, two-pronged fork with one arm much longer than the other, used to catch mail bags at stations where the train did not stop. When not in use both arms were carried against the side of the car. The long arm caught the mail sack hanging from a rack, and another lever allowed the operator to pull the pouch inside.

warming shelf: A narrow shelf above the fire door where a long-spouted copper can filled with melted tallow was kept for lubricating the sliding valves.

washout: A stop signal. At night the signaler swings a lantern in a wide semicircle across the track, and in the daytime he waves both arms in a downward arc.

waste: Tangled spun-cotton threads used to wipe oil from engines and also as packing in wheel journals after being soaked in oil.

watch: A work shift.

watch your pins: To be careful around dangerous stacks of rails, ties, or other stocks.

water up: To take on water.

way bill: A document, prepared by the carrier of a shipment, containing details about the shipment, the route, and the charges.

way car: A car of local freight. A caboose; this term was seldom applied to the caboose in the West but to the car used for local freight and kept on the head end of freight trains.

way-car bounce: A trip with only the engine and a way car; also called *way-car hop.*

way-car hop: See *way-car bounce.*

way mail: Mail to be delivered along the route.

wear brass buttons: An expression describing a conductor.

wear the blue: To be delayed for repairs by car inspectors; cars thus delayed are identified by a blue flag or a blue light.

wear the feather: Said of a plume of steam from a locomotive safety valve.

wear the green: To carry green signals. When trains are running in more than one section, all except the last train must display two green flags during the day and two green lights at night.

web: See *crank web.*

wedge: One of four large screws on the main rod

providing a wedge-type adjustment for taking up slack in the brass bearings.

weed bender: A cowboy with a shipment of cattle.

weeder: A section boss.

Westinghouse: An air brake.

wet mule in the firebox: A bad job of firing a loco-motive.

whale belly: A steel coal car with a drop bottom and curved sides.

whale 'em over the hill: To run a train at high speed.

whangdoodle: An outlying telephone.

wheel: To drive a locomotive at high speed.

wheel base: The distance between the first pair of locomotive wheels and the last pair of tender wheels.

wheel 'em: To run a train without braking. To haul at good speed. See *highball.*

wheel 'em up to the switch: To make a fast run to a switch. When the engineer did so, the front brake-man had to outrun the engine to throw the switch.

wheeler: A wheeled scraper used in building railroad grades.

wheelerman: A rear brakeman.

wheel monkey: A car inspector.

wheel stick: A stout pole used to elevate a car wheel in order to turn it.

When do you shine? A question meaning, "What time are you called for?"

whiffletree: A coupling.

whiskers: A man with many years of seniority.

WHISKY
>	*See* bust head, coffin varnish, panther sweat, stagger soup, tonsil paint.

whistle off: To sound the departure whistle, two short blasts.

whistle out a flag: To blow one long and three short blasts, signaling the rear brakeman to protect the rear of the train. It meant that he was to grab a red flag by day or a red lantern by night and run far enough behind the rear end to prevent a rear-end collision.

whistle pig: An engineer.

whistle post: A white post set alongside the track to signal the engineer to whistle for an approaching station, crossing, and so on.

whistle stop: A small station or town.

white-eye: A semaphore signal meaning a clear track ahead.

white feather: A plume of steam over the engine safety valve, indicating high boiler pressure.

white ribbon: A white flag. An extra train.

whitewash: Milk.

whiz: The air that operates the brakes.

Whyte classification: A classification of locomotives by wheel arrangements. For example, a locomotive with four guiding wheels, eight drivers, and two trailing wheels would be designated 4-8-2.

widen on her: To open the throttle to increase speed.

wigwag: A grade-crossing signal.

wildcat: To run an extra train or a locomotive without cars.

Willie: A waybill for a loaded car.

wind: An air brake.

windjammer: An air brake.

window music: The scenery the passenger sees on his travels.

wing her: To set the brakes violently.

wiper: A man hired to clean an engine just in off the road.

wire tapper: A telegraph operator.

wisdom box: A yardmaster's office.

wise guy: A station agent.

wolf: A nonbrotherhood man.

woodburner: An early-day engine that burned wood for fuel.

Wooten firebox: An engine firebox placed above the driving wheels. It provides a much larger grate area than its predecessors and is used on engines that burn anthracite coal. It is named for its inventor, John E. Wooten.

work car: To unload a storage mail car.

working mail: Mail in sacks to be sorted en route.

working steam: Said of a laboring locomotive.

work in the field: Said of a yard switchman who does not follow the engine.

WORK SHIFT

See tour, graveyard shift, gravy eye, trick, watch.

work the yards: To switch cars.

work train: A train of boxcars converted into living quarters for repair or maintenance crews. One car was fitted with bunks, two for kitchen and dining cars, and one for an office and bunks for the foreman. A flatcar or two are included for carrying wheelbarrows, shovels, and other tools.

work-water: The engineer operating the injector and watching the water glass or gauge cocks. Later it was the fireman's job.

wrapper sheets: The outside shell of the firebox, together with the metal sheets covering the lagging on the boiler.

WRECK

See big hook, bunch of thieves, cornfield meet, crack up, head-ender, head-on, hook, in the ditch, on the ground, on the ties, pile up, run in, smash up, stack up, tail-ender.

wrecking crane: A flatcar with a house at one end enclosing a vertical steam boiler, the engine, and a hoisting machine.

wrecking crew: A relief crew, so called because of the state of a car after it had been used by relief men.

wrench artist: A mechanic.

wrong iron: The main track on which the current of traffic is in the opposite direction.

wye: Tracks forming the letter Y, used for turning cars and engines where no turntable is available.

X: An empty car.
XXX: A bad order.

Y: See *wye.*

yard: A system of tracks used for storing cars or making up trains.

yard bull: A railroad detective who works in the yard.

yard clerk: A man who works in the yard office.

YARD CLERK
> *See* mud hop, number dummy, number grabber, paperweight, yard clerk.

yard dick: A railroad detective who works in the yard to protect property from theft or damage.

yard goose: A switchman.

yard goat: A switch engine.

yardman: See *yardmaster.*

yardmaster: A railroad man in charge of operations in a railroad yard; also called *yardman.*

YARDMASTER
> *See* back-porch yardmaster, bull goose, dinger, drill crew, general, groundhog, G.Y.M., jam buster, jiggerooski, knowledge box, master mind, Pocatello yardmaster, ringmaster, slave

driver, wisdom box, Y.M., yardman, yard-master.

YARDMASTER'S OFFICE
See beehive, G.Y.M., knowledge box.

Yellowstone-type engine: An articulated locomotive with a 2-8-8-4 wheel arrangement, used by the Northern Pacific beginning in 1929.

Y.M.: Short for *yardmaster (q.v.).*

young runner: A recently promoted engineer.

zoo: A caboose.

zookeeper: The gatekeeper at a passenger station. A *call boy (q.v.)*.

Zulu: An immigrant family traveling by rail with its household goods, farm implements, and livestock. These movers were common in the early days when men sought new homes in the West after reading the attractive literature put out by the railroads.

Zulu car: An immigrant car. See *Zulu*.

THE ENGINEER'S WHISTLE TALK

Some engineers, when returning to their home terminal, liked to play a tune or send a message (see
quill), on their whistle. Every toot had a meaning, and
every railroader had to learn to interpret this whistle
talk. As whistles were developed from simple quills
to as many as five in clusters fed by a single valve,
engineers found that they could produce tunes when
steam was admitted at different intensities. The
whistles of the early days were small and shrill and
offensive to the ear, but in time they evolved into
melodious, bell-type whistles. Below is a list of
whistle signals and their meanings:

One short toot: Apply brakes. Stop.
Two long: Release brakes. Proceed.
One long, three short: Flagman protect rear of train.
Four long: Flagman return from west or south.
Five long: Flagman return from east or north.
Three short, one long: Flagman protect front of train.
Two short: Answer any signal not otherwise provided
    for.
Three short: When standing, back up; when running,
    stop at the next passenger station.
Four short: call for signals.

Two long, one short, one long: Approaching highway crossing at grade (repeated until crossing is reached).

One extralong: Approaching station, junction, or railroad crossing.

Two long, one short: Approaching meeting or waiting point.

One short, one long: Inspect train line for leak or sticking brake.

One long, two short: (on single track) Attention of train crew of trains of the same class, inferior trains, and yard engines to signals displayed for a following section. If not answered by a train displaying the signals, stop and ascertain the cause; (on two or more tracks) to call the attention of trains of the same class, inferior trains moving in the same direction, and yard engines to signals displayed for a following section.

A succession of continued short toots: Persons or livestock on the track.

When the engineer wanted to flirt with a girl along the track or greet a fellow man, he gave two short toots as a recognition.

Sad to say for the railroad buff, the melodious whistle of the steam age has given way to the voice of the diesel, which is not as pleasing.